CAMBRIDGE | Discovery
EDUCATION

# UNLOCK

## LISTENING & SPEAKING SKILLS

**1**

N. M. White

CAMBRIDGE
UNIVERSITY PRESS

# CAMBRIDGE
## UNIVERSITY PRESS

University Printing House, Cambridge CB2 8BS, United Kingdom

One Liberty Plaza, 20th Floor, New York, NY 10006, USA

477 Williamstown Road, Port Melbourne, VIC 3207, Australia

4843/24, 2nd Floor, Ansari Road, Daryaganj, Delhi – 110002, India

79 Anson Road, #06–04/06, Singapore 079906

Cambridge University Press is part of the University of Cambridge.

It furthers the University's mission by disseminating knowledge in the pursuit of education, learning and research at the highest international levels of excellence.

www.cambridge.org
Information on this title: www.cambridge.org/9781107678101

First published 2014

20  19  18  17  16  15  14

Printed in Dubai by Oriental Press

*A catalogue record for this publication is available from the British Library*

ISBN 978-1-107-67810-1 Listening and Speaking 1 Student's Book with Online Workbook
ISBN 978-1-107-66211-7 Listening and Speaking 1 Teacher's Book with DVD
ISBN 978-1-107-61399-7 Reading and Writing 1 Student's Book with Online Workbook
ISBN 978-1-107-61401-7 Reading and Writing 1 Teacher's Book with DVD

Additional resources for this publication at www.cambridge.org/unlock

# CONTENTS

# MAP OF THE BOOK

| UNIT | VIDEO | LISTENING | VOCABULARY | |
|------|-------|-----------|------------|---|
| **1 PEOPLE**<br><br>Listening 1: Introductions (Communication studies)<br><br>Listening 2: Presentations about famous people (Celebrity studies) | The film makers | *Key listening skill*:<br>Understanding key vocabulary<br><br>Listening for main ideas<br>Listening for detail<br><br>*Pronunciation for listening*:<br>Syllable stress | Family<br>Jobs<br>Countries and nationalities | |
| **2 SEASONS**<br><br>Listening 1: A talk about three different places (Landscape architecture)<br><br>Listening 2: Presentations about landscapes (Meteorology) | Seasons in North America | *Key listening skill*:<br>Using visuals to predict content<br><br>Understanding key vocabulary<br>Listening for main ideas<br>Listening for detail<br><br>*Pronunciation for listening*:<br>Sentence stress | Months and seasons<br>Weather<br>Colours | |
| **3 LIFESTYLE**<br><br>Listening 1: Three conversations about different lifestyles (Sociology)<br><br>Listening 2: An interview (Anthropology) | The Bedouin | *Key listening skill*:<br>Listening for main ideas<br><br>Understanding key vocabulary<br>Listening for detail<br><br>*Pronunciation for listening*:<br>Intonation | Days of the week<br>Time expressions<br>Collocations for lifestyle (e.g. *download apps*, *go to the gym*, *have dinner with friends*) | |
| **4 PLACES**<br><br>Listening 1: Part of a geography seminar (Urban geography)<br><br>Listening 2: A guided tour (Tourism geography) | The Great Barrier Reef | *Key listening skill*:<br>Listening for detail<br><br>Understanding key vocabulary<br>Using your knowledge<br>Listening for main ideas<br><br>*Pronunciation for listening*:<br>Stress in determiners (*this*, *that*) | Vocabulary for places (e.g. *bank*, *bridge*, *library*, *mosque*)<br>Prepositions of place | |
| **5 SPORT**<br><br>Listening 1: A university lecture about sport (Sports science)<br><br>Listening 2: A student presentation about sport and exercise (Health sciences) | Free diving | *Key listening skill*:<br>Using your knowledge<br><br>Understanding key vocabulary<br>Listening for main ideas<br>Listening for detail<br><br>*Pronunciation for listening*:<br>Pronouncing clusters of consonants (e.g. *-gh*, *-ing*, *ph*, *ck*) | Vocabulary for sport<br>Sports collocations (e.g. *play tennis*, *go swimming*, *do karate*) | |

| GRAMMAR | CRITICAL THINKING | SPEAKING |
|---|---|---|
| Personal pronouns<br>Possessive adjectives<br>The verb *be* | Use ideas maps | ***Preparation for speaking***<br>Introducing and starting a talk<br>***Pronunciation for speaking***<br>Saying words and sentences in syllables<br>***Speaking task***<br>Tell your group about two famous people from your country. |
| *There is* and *There are*<br>Adjectives | Choose visuals for a talk | ***Preparation for speaking***<br>Describing photographs<br>***Pronunciation for speaking***<br>Word stress<br>***Speaking task***<br>Describe photographs of a landscape. |
| The present simple | Use surveys | ***Preparation for speaking***<br>Asking and answering questions<br>***Pronunciation for speaking***<br>Intonation in questions<br>***Speaking task***<br>Interview students for a survey. |
| The imperative | Interpret maps and give directions | ***Preparation for speaking***<br>Asking for and giving directions<br>***Pronunciation for speaking***<br>Pronunciation of phrases<br>***Speaking task***<br>Ask for and give directions. |
| Comparative adjectives | Use a table to make notes | ***Preparation for speaking***<br>Making comparisons and introducing a talk<br>***Pronunciation for speaking***<br>Weak vowel sounds<br>***Speaking task***<br>Compare different kinds of sport and exercise. |

| UNIT | VIDEO | LISTENING | VOCABULARY |
|------|-------|-----------|------------|
| **6 JOBS**<br><br>Listening 1: A formal conversation asking for advice (Careers guidance)<br><br>Listening 2: A job interview (Human resource management) | Fire rangers | *Key listening skill*:<br>Listening for opinion<br><br>Predicting content<br>Understanding key vocabulary<br>Listening for main ideas<br>Listening for detail<br><br>*Pronunciation for listening*:<br>Word stress | Vocabulary for jobs: suffixes<br>Adjectives for people (e.g. *good-looking, kind, polite, slim*)<br>Collocations for jobs (e.g. *build houses, do experiments, serve food*) |
| **7 HOME AND BUILDINGS**<br><br>Listening 1: A radio interview (Demography)<br><br>Listening 2: A discussion: ideas for a new building (Architecture) | Homes in Dharavi, India | *Key listening skill*:<br>Listening for reasons<br><br>Understanding key vocabulary<br>Listening for main ideas<br>Listening for detail<br><br>*Pronunciation for listening*:<br>Linking words | Vocabulary for rooms<br>Adjectives for furniture (e.g. *comfortable, wooden, glass*) |
| **8 FOOD AND CULTURE**<br><br>Listening 1: A university lecture about food in cities (Food studies)<br><br>Listening 2: A survey (Gastronomy) | Chinese food | *Key listening skill*:<br>Listening for numbers<br><br>Predicting content using visuals<br>Understanding key vocabulary<br>Listening for detail<br>Listening for main ideas<br><br>*Pronunciation for listening*:<br>Pronunciation of *-teen* and *-ty* numbers | Vocabulary for food |
| **9 ANIMALS**<br><br>Listening 1: A talk about orangutans (Animal behaviour)<br><br>Listening 2: A student talk about an animal from their country (Zoology) | Animals and people | *Key listening skill*:<br>Listening for definitions<br><br>Using your knowledge<br>Understanding key vocabulary<br>Listening for main ideas<br>Listening for detail<br><br>*Pronunciation for listening*:<br>Silent consonants | Vocabulary for animals |
| **10 TRANSPORT**<br><br>Listening 1: A discussion about Transport for London (Transport and logistics)<br><br>Listening 2: A debate about a transport problem (Urban planning) | Alaskan transport | *Key listening skill*:<br>Taking notes<br><br>Using your knowledge<br>Understanding key vocabulary<br>Predicting content using visuals<br>Listening for main ideas<br>Listening for detail<br><br>*Pronunciation for listening*:<br>Pronouncing years (e.g. *1994, nineteen ninety-four*) | Vocabulary for transport |

| GRAMMAR | CRITICAL THINKING | SPEAKING |
|---|---|---|
| *have/has to* | Choose criteria | **Preparation for speaking**<br>Asking for and giving reasons<br><br>**Pronunciation for speaking**<br>Pronouncing consonants in *have to, have, has to, has* (e.g. /f/, /v/, /z/, /s/)<br><br>**Speaking task**<br>Choose a person for a job. |
| *should* | Find reasons for and against | **Preparation for speaking**<br>Asking for and giving opinions<br>Agreeing and disagreeing<br><br>**Speaking task**<br>Discuss ideas for a new building. |
| Countable and uncountable nouns (with *some, any, much, many*) | Use pie charts | **Preparation for speaking**<br>Introducing a report<br>Talking about the results<br><br>**Pronunciation for speaking**<br>Sentence stress: emphasis<br><br>**Speaking Task**<br>Report the results of a survey. |
| Definitions (e.g. *a kind of, that means, is the name for*) | Use online translation tools and dictionaries | **Preparation for speaking**<br>Introducing a topic<br>Using questions in a talk<br><br>**Pronunciation for speaking**<br>Pauses<br><br>**Speaking task**<br>Describe an animal. |
| The past simple | Use flow charts | **Preparation for speaking**<br>Describing a topic<br>Describing a problem<br>Describing a solution<br>Describing results<br><br>**Pronunciation for speaking**<br>Past simple endings: /t/, /d/, /ɪd/<br><br>**Speaking task**<br>Describe a solution to a transport problem. |

# **UNL⌀CK** UNIT STRUCTURE

The units in *Unlock Listening and Speaking Skills* are carefully scaffolded so that students build the skills and language they need throughout the unit in order to produce a successful Speaking task.

**UNLOCK YOUR KNOWLEDGE** | Encourages discussion around the theme of the unit with inspiration from interesting questions and striking visuals.

**WATCH AND LISTEN** | Features an engaging and motivating *Discovery Education™* video which generates interest in the topic.

**LISTENING 1** | Provides information about the topic and practises pre-listening, while listening and post-listening skills. This section also includes a focus on a pronunciation feature which will further enhance listening comprehension.

**LANGUAGE DEVELOPMENT** | Practises the vocabulary and grammar from Listening 1 and pre-teaches the vocabulary and grammar from Listening 2.

**LISTENING 2** | Provides a different angle on the topic and serves as a model for the speaking task.

**CRITICAL THINKING** | Contains brainstorming, categorising, evaluative and analytical tasks as preparation for the speaking task.

**PREPARATION FOR SPEAKING / SPEAKING SKILLS** | Presents and practises functional language, pronunciation and speaking strategies for the speaking task.

**SPEAKING TASK** | Uses the skills and strategies learnt over the course of the unit to produce a presentational or interactional speaking task.

**OBJECTIVES REVIEW** | Allows learners to assess how well they have mastered the skills covered in the unit.

**WORDLIST** | Includes the key vocabulary from the unit.

This is the unit's main learning objective. It gives learners the opportunity to use all the language and skills they have learnt in the unit.

# UNL⦶CK MOTIVATION

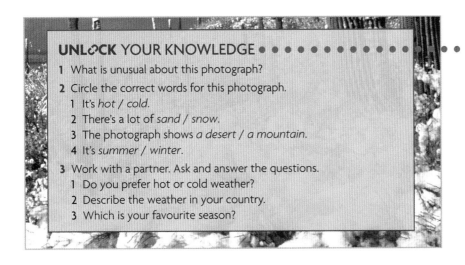

## UNL⦶CK YOUR KNOWLEDGE • • • • • • • • • • • • • • •

1 What is unusual about this photograph?

2 Circle the correct words for this photograph.
  1 It's *hot / cold*.
  2 There's a lot of *sand / snow*.
  3 The photograph shows *a desert / a mountain*.
  4 It's *summer / winter*.

3 Work with a partner. Ask and answer the questions.
  1 Do you prefer hot or cold weather?
  2 Describe the weather in your country.
  3 Which is your favourite season?

### PERSONALIZE

*Unlock* encourages students to bring their own knowledge, experiences and opinions to the topics. This **motivates** students to relate the topics to their own contexts.

### DISCOVERY EDUCATION™ VIDEO

**Thought-provoking** videos from *Discovery Education*™ are included in every unit throughout the course to introduce topics, promote discussion and motivate learners. The videos provide a new angle on a wide range of academic subjects.

" The video was excellent! It helped with raising students' interest in the topic. It was well-structured and the language level was appropriate.

Maria Agata Szczerbik,
United Arab Emirates University,
Al-Ain, UAE "

# UNL⌀CK CRITICAL THINKING

> [...] with different styles of visual aids such as mind maps, grids, tables and pictures, this [critical thinking] section [provides] very crucial tools that can encourage learners to develop their speaking skills.
>
> Dr. Panidnad Chulerk, Rangit University, Thailand

## BLOOM'S TAXONOMY

CREATE — create, invent, plan, compose, construct, design, imagine

decide, rate, choose, recommend, justify, assess, prioritize — EVALUATE

ANALYZE — explain, contrast, examine, identify, investigate, categorize

show, complete, use, classify, examine, illustrate, solve — APPLY

UNDERSTAND — compare, discuss, restate, predict, translate, outline

name, describe, relate, find, list, write, tell — REMEMBER

## BLOOM'S TAXONOMY

The Critical thinking sections in *Unlock* are based on Benjamin Bloom's classification of learning objectives. This ensures learners develop their **lower-** and **higher-order thinking skills**, ranging from demonstrating **knowledge** and **understanding** to in-depth **evaluation**.
The margin headings in the Critical thinking sections highlight the exercises which develop Bloom's concepts.

## LEARN TO THINK

Learners engage in **evaluative** and **analytical tasks** that are designed to ensure they do all of the thinking and information-gathering required for the end-of-unit speaking task.

## CRITICAL THINKING

UNDERSTAND

At the end of this unit, you are going to do the speaking task below.

Tell your group about two famous people from your country.

### Ideas maps

An ideas map helps you think about the topic and organize information about it. It also helps you to remember key information and vocabulary.

1 Look at the ideas maps below and answer the questions.

1 What is the main topic of each map?
2 What other topics can you find in the maps?
3 What language information can you find in the maps?
4 Which ideas map do you prefer? Why?

Map 1

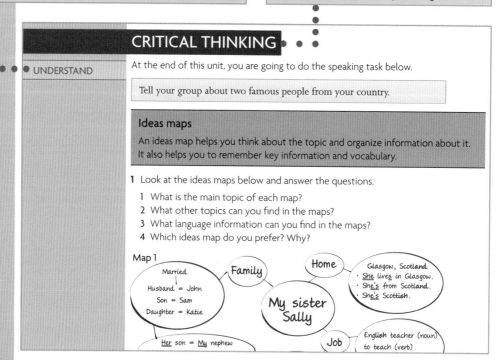

# UNLOCK RESEARCH

## THE CAMBRIDGE LEARNER CORPUS ⊙

The **Cambridge Learner Corpus** is a bank of official Cambridge English exam papers. Our exclusive access means we can use the corpus to carry out unique research and identify the most common errors that learners make. That information is used to ensure the *Unlock* syllabus teaches the most **relevant language**.

## THE WORDS YOU NEED

Language Development sections provide vocabulary and grammar-building tasks that are further practised in the ⊙**UNLOCK ONLINE** Workbook. The glossary provides definitions and pronunciation, and the end-of-unit wordlists provide useful summaries of key vocabulary.

## ⊙ LANGUAGE DEVELOPMENT

### VOCABULARY FOR JOBS

EXPLANATION

**Suffixes**

We can use a suffix to make new words for jobs.

    music + -ian = musician
    police + -man = policeman
    build + -er = builder

**1** Work with a partner. Think of more jobs for each suffix.

UNDERSTANDING KEY VOCABULARY

## PREPARING TO LISTEN

**1** You are going to listen to an interview on the radio. Before you listen, match the pairs.

| | |
|---|---|
| 1 A psychologist | a manages a restaurant. |
| 2 An architect | b studies how people think. |
| 3 A restaurant manager | c designs buildings. |

EXPLANATION

**Linking words**

Link consonant sounds to vowel sounds.

    Krishna lives_in_India.
    Because_it's_a good_idea.

UNLOCK ONLINE

## ACADEMIC LANGUAGE

Unique research using the **Cambridge English Corpus** has been carried out into academic language, in order to provide learners with relevant, academic vocabulary from the start (CEFR A1 and above). This addresses a gap in current academic vocabulary mapping and ensures learners are presented with carefully selected words which they will find essential during their studies.

## PRONUNCIATION FOR LISTENING

This unique feature of *Unlock* focuses on aspects of pronunciation which may inhibit listening comprehension. This means that learners are primed to understand detail and nuance while listening.

> " The language development is clear and the strong lexical focus is positive as learners feel they make more progress when they learn more vocabulary.
>
> Colleen Wackrow,
> Princess Nourah Bint Abdulrahman University, Al-Riyadh, Kingdom of Saudi Arabia "

# **UNL⊙CK** SOLUTIONS

## FLEXIBLE

*Unlock* is available in a range of print and digital components, so teachers can mix and match according to their requirements.

## **UNL⊙CK** ONLINE WORKBOOKS

The **UNL⊙CK ONLINE** Workbooks are accessed via activation codes packaged with the Student's Books. These **easy-to-use** workbooks provide interactive exercises, games, tasks, and further practice of the language and skills from the Student's Books in the Cambridge LMS, an engaging and modern learning environment.

## CAMBRIDGE LEARNING MANAGEMENT SYSTEM (LMS)

The Cambridge LMS provides teachers with the ability to track learner progress and save valuable time thanks to automated marking functionality. Blogs, forums and other tools are also available to facilitate communication between students and teachers.

## **UNL⊙CK** EBOOKS

The *Unlock* Student's Books and Teacher's Books are also available as interactive eBooks. With answers and *Discovery Education*™ videos embedded, the eBooks provide a great alternative to the printed materials.

- Each level of *Unlock* consists of two Student's Books: **Reading & Writing** and **Listening & Speaking** and an accompanying Teacher's Book for each. Online Workbooks are packaged with each Student's Book.
- Complete course audio is available to download from www.cambridge.org/unlock
- Look out for the ⟨UNL⦿CK ONLINE⟩ symbols in the Student's Books which indicate that additional practice of that skill or language area is available in the Online Workbook.
- Every *Unlock* Student's Book is delivered both in print format and as an interactive **eBook for tablet devices**.
- The *Unlock* Teacher's Books contain additional speaking tasks, tests, teaching tips and research projects for students.
- *Presentation Plus* **software for interactive whiteboards** is available for all Student's Books.

## LISTENING AND SPEAKING

| | | | | |
|---|---|---|---|---|
| Student's Book and Online Workbook Pack* | 978-1-107-67810-1 | 978-1-107-68232-0 | 978-1-107-68728-8 | 978-1-107-63461-9 |
| Teacher's Book with DVD* | 978-1-107-66211-7 | 978-1-107-64280-5 | 978-1-107-68154-5 | 978-1-107-65052-7 |
| Presentation Plus (interactive whiteboard software) | 978-1-107-66424-1 | 978-1-107-69582-5 | 978-1-107-63543-2 | 978-1-107-64381-9 |

*eBooks available from **www.cambridge.org/unlock**

The complete course audio is available from
**www.cambridge.org/unlock**

## READING AND WRITING

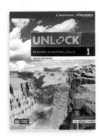   

| | | | | |
|---|---|---|---|---|
| Student's Book and Online Workbook Pack* | 978-1-107-61399-7 | 978-1-107-61400-0 | 978-1-107-61526-7 | 978-1-107-61525-0 |
| Teacher's Book with DVD* | 978-1-107-61401-7 | 978-1-107-61403-1 | 978-1-107-61404-8 | 978-1-107-61409-3 |
| Presentation Plus (interactive whiteboard software) | 978-1-107-63800-6 | 978-1-107-65605-5 | 978-1-107-67624-4 | 978-1-107-68245-0 |

*eBooks available from **www.cambridge.org/unlock**

## LEARNING OBJECTIVES

| | |
|---|---|
| Watch and listen | Watch and understand a video about film makers |
| Listening skills | Understand key vocabulary |
| Speaking skills | Vocabulary for countries and nationalities; phrases for introducing and starting a talk; vocabulary for people |
| Speaking task | Talk about famous people from your country |

# UNLOCK YOUR KNOWLEDGE

Work with a partner. Ask and answer the questions.

1 What can you see in the photograph?
2 What is happening?
• 3 Why do people enjoy events like this?

# WATCH AND LISTEN

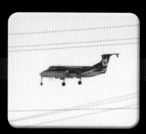

## PREPARING TO WATCH

**1** You are going to watch a video about some people who are making a nature film. They are in Alaska. Match the words from the box with the pictures below (1–4).

equipment   helicopter   seal   tracks

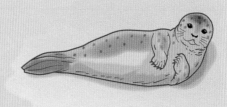

1 _____

2 _____

3 _____

4 _____

**2** Read the sentences about film makers and circle the correct answers.

1 A cameraman *takes pictures / buys films*.
2 A sound man *writes the music / records what he can hear*.
3 An assistant *helps / teaches* other people.
4 A producer *buys / sells* things for the film makers.
5 A presenter *plans the film / speaks to the camera*.
6 The crew is everybody who is *making / watching* the film.

## WHILE WATCHING

**3** ▶ Watch the video and answer the questions.

1 How do the film makers travel in Alaska?
2 What do they want to film?
3 What do they see from the helicopter?

UNDERSTANDING
MAIN IDEAS

**4** ▶ Watch again. Circle the correct answers.

1 Where does Glenn make films? *All over Alaska / All over the world*
2 How many people live in Kaktovik? *Three hundred / Four hundred*
3 How much equipment does the crew have? *A little / A lot*
4 How many polar bears do they see? *Three / Four*
5 Where do the crew film the polar bears? *On the ice / From the helicopter*

UNDERSTANDING
DETAIL

## DISCUSSION

**5** Work in groups. Ask and answer the questions.

1 Which job in a film crew is the best, do you think?
2 Would you like to make nature films? If yes, where?
3 Would you like to go to places like Alaska? Why? / Why not?
4 Would you like to make other kinds of film?

# LISTENING 1

## Understanding key vocabulary

Before you listen, try to understand the key vocabulary in the Preparing to listen exercises. These words will help you understand the main ideas of the recording.

## PREPARING TO LISTEN

**UNDERSTANDING KEY VOCABULARY**

**1** You are going to listen to four students talk about somebody they know. Before you listen, read about two other students. Then write words from the texts in the table below.

My name's Fahd and I'm from Saudi Arabia. I'm 19 and I'm a student. I have a brother and three sisters. My family's from Riyadh, but my brother has a house in Jeddah. He's a doctor there.

My name's Li Yu Lin and I'm from China. I'm 21 and I'm a student. I have one brother. We have a hotel in Shanghai. My mother and father are the managers.

| topic | key vocabulary |
|---|---|
| family | brother, ... |
| occupations | student, ... |
| countries | Saudi Arabia, ... |

## PRONUNCIATION FOR LISTENING

**2** 🔊 **1.1** How many syllables do these words have? Listen and write 1, 2 or 3 in the boxes.

1 introduce ☐    4 Turkey ☐    7 study ☐    10 producer ☐
2 please ☐    5 twenty ☐    8 business ☐
3 Peru ☐    6 eighteen ☐    9 computer ☐

EXPLANATION

## Stress on one syllable in a word

When a word has more than one syllable, one syllable in the word has more stress than the others. We say it in a longer, louder way than the other syllables. The stressed syllables in these words are underlined.

<u>bro</u>-ther      <u>ma</u>-na-ger      oc-cu-<u>pa</u>-tion

**3** 🔊**1.1** Listen again. Underline the stressed syllables.

# WHILE LISTENING

**4** 🔊**1.2** Listen to four students. Match the countries to the people.

LISTENING FOR
MAIN IDEAS

Peru   Japan   Turkey   United Arab Emirates

1 Hussain _____

2 Nehir _____

3 Carlos _____

4 Koko _____

**5** 🔊**1.2** Listen again. Circle the correct answers to the questions.

1 They talk about
   a teachers in their school.
   b students in their class.
   c their friends at home.

2 They tell us about these people's
   a families.
   b holidays.
   c homes.

3 They also tell us what these people want to
   a do in the holidays.
   b change at home.
   c study at university.

**6** 🔊 **1.2** Write T (true) or F (false) next to the sentences. Then listen again and check your answers.

1 Koko is 18.  ____
2 Her father is a TV presenter.  ____
3 Hussain is 20.  ____
4 He has two brothers and a sister.  ____
5 Nehir has a brother.  ____
6 Her family has a hotel.  ____
7 Carlos is 18.  ____
8 His mother is a teacher.  ____

**7** Work with a partner. Ask and answer questions about the people in Exercise 4.

1 What's his/her name?
2 How old is he/she?
3 What does he/she do?
4 Where's he/she from?
5 Does he/she have any brothers and sisters?
6 What does he/she want to do in the future?

## DISCUSSION

**8** Work with a partner. Talk about

- your name (*I'm ...*).
- your occupation (*I'm a(n) ...*).
- your country and hometown (*I'm from ...*).
- about people in your family (*I have ... , My father's a ... , My mother's a ...*).
- your plans for the future (*I want to ...*).

**9** Work in groups. Talk about your partner in Exercise 8.

This is ... He's/She's [18]. He's/She's from [Turkey]. He's/She's a [student]. He's/She's from [Ankara]. He/She has [two sisters]. He/She wants to [study Business at university].

**UNL⌀CK** LISTENING AND SPEAKING SKILLS 1

# ⊙ LANGUAGE DEVELOPMENT

## PERSONAL PRONOUNS AND POSSESSIVE ADJECTIVES

1 Look at the sentences from Listening 1. The personal pronouns are underlined. The possessive adjectives are circled.

> I'm Carlos.
> She's a student in (our) class. (Her) family's from Sapporo.
> He's from the UAE. (His) family's from Al-Ain.

Complete the table below with the personal pronouns and possessive adjectives from the box.

> my   your   its   we   their

| personal pronouns | possessive adjectives |
|---|---|
| I | (1) _____ |
| you | (2) _____ |
| he | his |
| she | her |
| it | (3) _____ |
| (4) _____ | our |
| they | (5) _____ |

We use personal pronouns before a verb.

   I'm Carlos. She's 18.

We use possessive adjectives before a noun.

   My name is Fahd. Her family has a hotel.

2 Write the correct possessive adjectives in the gaps.

   1 This is Koko's book. ➔ This is _____her_____ book.
   2 This is my brother's car. ➔ This is _____ car.
   3 This is our daughter's school. ➔ This is _____ school.
   4 This is my uncle and aunt's house. ➔ This is _____ house.
   5 This is my town and my family's town. ➔ This is _____ town.

**3** Circle the correct answers.

    **1** *She / Her* name's Kerry.

    **2** Is this *you / your* house?

    **3** This bag is nice. Is *it /its* new?

    **4** *He / His* is the manager of a shop.

    **5** *They / Their* teacher is from Egypt.

    **6** I'd like to study at this university. *It /Its* courses are very good.

    **7** *I / My* have a problem with *I / my* computer.

    **8** *We / Our* have a restaurant in *we / our* hotel.

## THE VERB *BE*

**4** 🔊**13** Listen and circle the forms you hear.

    **A**

| | |
|---|---|
| **Kerry:** | (1) *That is / That's* a lovely photograph, Mehmet. |
| **Mehmet:** | Thank you. (2) *It is / It's* a photograph of my friend. |
| **Kerry:** | (3) *What is / What's* her name? |
| **Mehmet:** | Meral. |
| **Kerry:** | Is she from Turkey? |
| **Mehmet:** | Yes, but she (4) *is not / isn't* from Ankara like me. (5) *She is / She's* from Izmir. |

    **B**

| | |
|---|---|
| **Ryo:** | Excuse me, Kerry. Are you from London? |
| **Kerry:** | No, no, (6) *I am not / I'm not* from England. (7) *I am / I'm* from Australia. But my grandparents are English. They (8) *are not / aren't* from London. (9) *They are / They're* from Manchester. |
| **Ryo:** | Are your parents Australian? |
| **Kerry:** | Yes – and my sisters. (10) *We are / We're* all Australian. |

**EXPLANATION**

The verb *be* has three present forms: *am* (*'m*), *is* (*'s*) and *are* (*'re*).

    I'm from Australia. (*'m = am*)

    It's a photograph of my friend. (*'s = is*)

    We're all Australian. They're from Manchester. (*'re = are*)

We add *not* to make the negative.

    I'm not from England. (*'m not = am not*)

    She isn't from Ankara. (*isn't / 's not = is not*)

    They aren't from London. (*'re not / aren't = are not*)

    You're not / You aren't

    He's/She's not / He/She isn't

    We're not / We aren't

    They're not / They aren't

The verb is before the subject in questions.

    What's her name? Is she from Turkey? Are you from London?

**5** Complete the dialogue with the correct form of *be*. Add *not* if necessary.

A: (1)_____ Are _____ you from Cairo?

B: No, I (2)_____ Egyptian. I (3)_____ from Abu Dhabi.

A: Who (4)_____ these people in this photograph? (5)_____
they your brothers?

B: No, they (6)_____ my friends. They (7)_____ from Abu Dhabi.
Hüsnü (8)_____ from Turkey, and Tariq (9)_____ from Oman.

A: (10)_____ they students?

B: Yes. We (11)_____ all students at the same college.

**6** Work with a partner. Practise the dialogue. Give answers that are true
for you.

## LISTENING 2

### PREPARING TO LISTEN

UNDERSTANDING
KEY VOCABULARY

**1** You are going to listen to two students talk
about famous people from their countries.
Who can you see in the photographs?
What are their jobs? Where are they from?

a

b

c

d

e

f

**2** Match the words (1–6) to a photograph (a–f).

1 fashion designer ☐ 4 businessman ☐
2 sportswoman ☐ 5 basketball player ☐
3 businesswoman ☐ 6 scientist ☐

**3** 🔊14 Listen to the words in Exercise 2. Write the number of syllables
in each word next to it. Then listen again and underline the stressed
syllables.

## WHILE LISTENING

**4** 🔊 **1.5** Listen to two students, Marie and Clare, talk about famous people from their countries. These people are in the photographs in Exercise 1. Answer the questions.

1 Where's Marie from?
2 Which two people does she talk about?
3 Where's Clare from?
4 Which two people does she talk about?

**5** 🔊 **1.5** Complete the table below by matching the sentences (1–10) with the people. Then listen again and check.

1 Her father's from Jamaica.
2 His wife's a scientist.
3 He's from the United States.
4 Her parents are from Panama.
5 She has a lot of medals.
6 He's from the United Kingdom.
7 She's from the United States.
8 She's from the United Kingdom.
9 His parents are computer scientists.
10 He has a Nobel Prize.

|          | Marie | Clare |
|----------|-------|-------|
| Person 1 |       | 1,    |
| Person 2 |       |       |

## DISCUSSION

**6** Work with a partner. Ask and answer questions about photographs b and e.

Student A: Go to page 195.
Student B: Go to page 197.

# CRITICAL THINKING

At the end of this unit, you are going to do the speaking task below.

Tell your group about two famous people from your country.

## Ideas maps

An ideas map helps you think about the topic and organize information about it. It also helps you to remember key information and vocabulary.

1 Look at the ideas maps below and answer the questions.

UNDERSTAND

1 What is the main topic of each map?
2 What other topics can you find in the maps?
3 What language information can you find in the maps?
4 Which map has pictures and colours?
5 Which ideas map do you prefer? Why?

Map 1

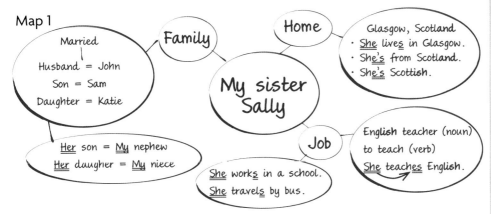

Map 2

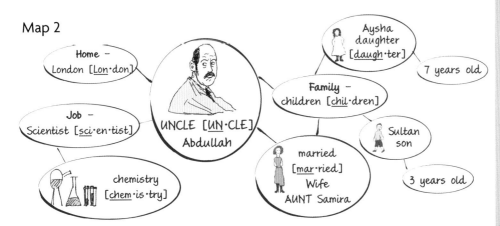

2 Choose an ideas map and describe the person to your partner.

**3** Make an ideas map about somebody in your family.

1 Write the name of the person in the centre.

2 Think about the person's family, occupation and home. Write key words for these areas (for example, 1 brother, 1 sister). Join them to the person's name.

3 Write about the key words (for example, 25 and 21; chef in hotel; student).

4 Write language information about the words in (2) and (3) above.

**4** Work with a partner. Ask and answer questions about the people in your ideas maps.

- Who's the person in your ideas map?
- Is he/she your [father/mother/brother/sister/cousin, etc.]?
- Where's he/she from?
- What does he/she do?
- How old is he/she?

**5** Work in groups. Tell the group about the person in your ideas map.

My ideas map is about ...

**6** Look at other people's ideas maps. Are they easy to understand? What colours are in them?

# SPEAKING

## PREPARATION FOR SPEAKING

### COUNTRIES AND NATIONALITIES

**1** Work with a partner. Complete the table on the next page with words for nationalities.

Student A: Go to page 194.
Student B: Go to page 196.

**2** Write words from the table in the gaps.

1 Fatma Al Nabhani is a famous _____ tennis player.
2 Ana García is from _____ .
3 Karim Abdel Aziz is an _____ actor.
4 Haruki Murakami is from _____ .
5 Lin Dan is a famous _____ badminton player.
6 Majid Al Futtaim is a famous _____ businessman.

| name | country | nationality |
|------|---------|-------------|
| Ana García | Mexico | (1) |
| Eunseong Kim | South Korea | South Korean |
| Tim Berners-Lee | Britain | British |
| Fatma Al Nabhani | Oman | (2) |
| Karim Abdel Aziz | Egypt | (3) |
| Lin Dan | China | Chinese |
| Majid Al Futtaim | the UAE | (4) |
| Haruki Murakami | Japan | (5) |
| Zeynep Ahunbay | Turkey | (6) |

## INTRODUCING AND STARTING A TALK

3  🔊16  Circle the correct phrases. Then listen and check.

1 _____ about two famous people from Mexico.
   a  I'm going to tell for you
   b  I'm going to tell you
   c  I'm going to tell

2 One person is _____ and one person is _____ .
   a  a famous woman ... a famous man
   b  famous woman ... famous man
   c  the famous woman ... the famous man

3 Ana García is _____ .
   a  famous Mexican chef
   b  a famous Mexican chef
   c  the famous Mexican chef

4 _____ Carlos Slim.
   a  It has
   b  This has
   c  This is

5 _____ a famous Mexican businessman.
   a  His is
   b  She's
   c  He's

## KEY VOCABULARY FOR PEOPLE

**4** Look at the words for some occupations. Add other words from this unit to the table.

| verb + -er/-r | verb + -or | noun + -er | noun + -ist |
|---|---|---|---|
| write: writer | act: actor | football: footballer | art: artist |
| dance: dancer | direct: director | garden: gardener | journal: journalist |
| sing: singer | | | |
| paint: painter | | | |
| manage: manager | | | |
| | | | |
| | | | |
| | | | |
| | | | |
| | | | |

## PRONUNCIATION FOR SPEAKING

### Saying words and sentences in syllables

To help say a word or sentence, start with the last syllable. This helps us put the stress in the correct place.

er
ball–er
<u>foot</u>–ball–er

We do the same with sentences to show the important words.

**5** 🔊 **1.7** Listen, read and repeat.

- er   <u>sign</u>-er   de-<u>sign</u>-er
- mous de-<u>sign</u>-er   <u>fa</u>-mous de-<u>sign</u>-er
- a <u>fa</u>-mous de-<u>sign</u>-er   she's a <u>fam</u>-ous de-<u>sign</u>-er

**6** 🔊 **1.8** Listen and repeat.

1 I'm going to <u>tell</u> you about two <u>fa</u>mous <u>peo</u>ple from <u>E</u>gypt.
2 Karim Abdel Aziz is a famous actor.
3 Carmen Suleiman's a famous singer.
4 Karim's father is Mohammed Abdel Aziz.
5 He's a film director.
6 Karim's aunt is Samira Muhsin.
7 She's an actor.

**7** 🔊 **1.8** <u>Underline</u> the stressed syllables in the sentences in Exercise 6. Then listen and repeat again.

**8** Change the sentences so they are true about people from your country.

*I'm going to tell you about two famous people from China.*
*Lin Dan's a famous badminton player.*

**9** Practise saying your sentences.

## SPEAKING TASK

**1** You are going to tell your group about two famous people, and listen to other students. Then your group is going to choose the famous person that you would like to meet.

- Think of two famous people and make an ideas map for each person.
- Find information about each person and a photograph on the internet.
- Include information about the person's country, occupation, age and parents.

**2** Write an introduction for your talk.

Hello! I'm _____ (*your name*) and I'm from _____ (*your city/country*).
I'm going to tell you about two famous people from my country.

**3** Write your talk. Use the information in your ideas map.

_____ (*name of Person 1*) is a famous _____ (*nationality*) _____ (*occupation*), and _____ (*name of Person 2*) is a famous _____ (*nationality*) _____ (*occupation*).

_____ (*name of Person 1*) is _____ (*age*). His/Her father is _____ (*name*). He's a/an _____ (*occupation*). His/Her mother is _____ (*name*). She's a/an _____ (*occupation*).

**4** Work in small groups. Talk about famous people from your country. Show people in your group your photographs. When you listen to other students, make notes in the chart about each person.

|  | person 1 | person 2 | person 3 | person 4 | person 5 | person 6 |
|---|---|---|---|---|---|---|
| name |  |  |  |  |  |  |
| country |  |  |  |  |  |  |
| occupation |  |  |  |  |  |  |
| age |  |  |  |  |  |  |
| family |  |  |  |  |  |  |

**5** Talk in your group. Which person would you like to meet? Why? Tell the class.

| TASK CHECKLIST | ✔ |
|---|---|
| Did you talk about two famous people from your country? |  |
| Did you make an ideas map? |  |
| Did you find key vocabulary for the people? |  |
| Did you use syllables and stress correctly? |  |

## OBJECTIVES REVIEW

*I can ...*

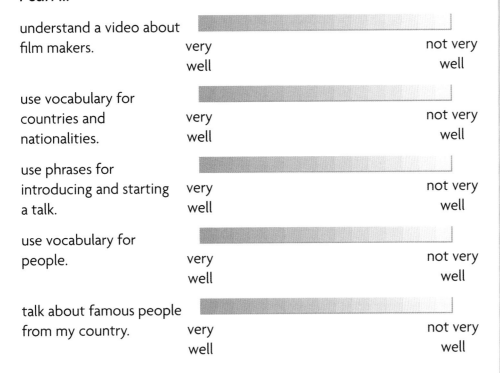

| | | |
|---|---|---|
| understand a video about film makers. | very well | not very well |
| use vocabulary for countries and nationalities. | very well | not very well |
| use phrases for introducing and starting a talk. | very well | not very well |
| use vocabulary for people. | very well | not very well |
| talk about famous people from my country. | very well | not very well |

## WORDLIST

| UNIT VOCABULARY | |
|---|---|
| artist (n) | father (n) |
| basketball player (n) | job (n) |
| brother (n) | journalist (n) |
| businessman (n) | mother (n) |
| businesswoman (n) | name (n) |
| city (n) | scientist (n) |
| country (n) | singer (n) |
| dancer (n) | sister (n) |
| doctor (n) | sportswoman (n) |
| family (n) | teacher (n) |
| famous (adj) | writer (n) |
| fashion designer (n) | |

## LEARNING OBJECTIVES

| Watch and listen | Watch and understand a video about weather |
| --- | --- |
| Listening skills | Use visuals to predict content |
| Speaking skills | Phrases with *there is / there are*; adjectives |
| Speaking task | Describe photographs of a landscape |

## UNLØCK YOUR KNOWLEDGE

1 What is unusual about this photograph?

2 Circle the correct words for this photograph.
  1 It's *hot / cold*.
  2 There's a lot of *sand / snow*.
  3 The photograph shows *a desert / a mountain*.
  4 It's *summer / winter*.

3 Work with a partner. Ask and answer the questions.
  1 Do you prefer hot or cold weather?
  2 Describe the weather in your country.
  3 Which is your favourite season?

# WATCH AND LISTEN

## PREPARING TO WATCH

**1** Write the words from the box next to the correct picture.

> flowers   fruit   plants   snow   a storm   vegetables

a _____   b _____   c _____

d _____   e _____   f _____

**2** Work with a partner. Ask and answer the questions.

1 How many seasons are there in your country?
2 In your country, when
   a does it rain?
   b does it snow?
   c can you see storms?
   d do fruit and vegetables grow?
   e do plants and flowers grow?

**3** Look at the diagram. Write a, b, c, d or e in statements 1–4.

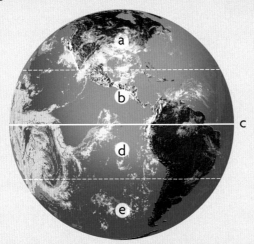

1 The weather is usually hot and sunny in <u>b, c, d</u> .
2 Countries in _____ have snow in winter.
3 Places in _____ have two seasons: a dry season and a rainy season.
4 Countries in _____ have four seasons.

## WHILE WATCHING

**4** ▶ Watch the video. Which parts of the diagram (a–e) show

1 the *equator*?
2 the *Tropic of Cancer*?
3 the *Tropic of Capricorn*?

**5** ▶ Watch again. Then match the seasons (1–4) to the statements about
weather in North America and Canada (a–j).

| | |
|---|---|
| 1 spring | a It is hot and sunny. |
| 2 summer  *a, ...* | b Trees change colour. |
| 3 autumn | c There are storms. |
| 4 winter | d There is snow in the cities. |
| | e Fruit and vegetables grow. |
| | f There's a lot of rain and sun. |
| | g It is dangerous for cars. |
| | h There's no school. |
| | i Plants and flowers grow. |
| | j Many people travel to the tropics. |

## DISCUSSION

**6** Discuss the questions.

1 Does it snow in your country? If yes, do you like snow? If no, would
you like to have snow in your country?
2 Can people go skiing in countries with no snow? Where? How?

## PREPARING TO LISTEN

UNDERSTANDING
KEY VOCABULARY

**1** You are going to listen to a talk about three different places. Match the pairs.

| | |
|---|---|
| 1 sky | **a** hot |
| 2 inside | **b** sea |
| 3 cold | **c** ugly |
| 4 summer | **d** man-made |
| 5 beautiful | **e** outside |
| 6 natural | **f** winter |

**2** Circle the correct word.

1 Dubai's *hot / cold* in July.
2 Canada has a lot of snow in *summer / winter*.
3 Cities are *natural / man-made* places.
4 We get snow when it's *hot / cold* here.
5 I don't like cities. I think they are *beautiful / ugly* places.
6 I like to stay at home when there is snow *inside / outside*.
7 There are no clouds in the *sky / sea* today.
8 'This is a photograph of my house.'
   'Oh! It's lovely – it's really *beautiful / ugly*.'
9 Mountains and forests are *natural / man-made* places.
10 It's starting to rain and I don't want to get wet – I think we should go *inside / outside*.
11 Many people like to swim in the *sky / sea*.
12 They have the World Skiing Championships in *summer / winter* every four years.

### Using visuals to predict content

*Visuals* can be photographs, pictures, graphs or tables. Use visuals to help you understand the topic and important ideas.

USING VISUALS TO
PREDICT CONTENT

**3** Look at the photographs (a–c) and answer the questions.

1 Would you like to visit any of these places? Why? / Why not?
2 Which are hot places?
3 Which have a beach?
4 What season can you see in each?
5 Which are cold places?
6 Which photographs have rocks or mountains?
7 Which photographs have sand?

a

Henry Doorly Zoo,
Omaha, Nebraska, US

b

Snow Centre, Hemel
Hempstead, England

c

Seagaia Ocean Dome,
Miyazaki, Japan

EXPLANATION

### Sentence stress

We stress important words in a sentence. Important words can be:

- <u>nouns</u>: *Dubai, July, Canada, lot, snow, winter, cities, places*
- (adjectives): *hot, man-made, cold*
- verbs (but not *be*): *has, get*

Dubai's (hot) in July.
Canada has a lot of snow in winter.
Cities are (man-made) places.
We get snow when it's (cold) here.

## PRONUNCIATION FOR LISTENING

4 🔊 2.1 Listen to sentences 1–5 and

- underline the nouns.
- circle the adjectives.
- highlight the verbs (but not *be*).

1 Today, I want to look at something new.
2 Take a look at photograph 1.
3 There's a beautiful beach next to a blue sea.
4 It's winter and there's a mountain.
5 It's hot and there's sand and there are rocks.

## WHILE LISTENING

5 🔊 2.2 Listen to a talk about three different places. Put the
photographs (a–c) in the correct order. Write 1–3 in the boxes.

6 What is unusual about these photographs?

LISTENING FOR
MAIN IDEAS

UNLOCK
ONLINE

**7** 🔊 2.2 Listen again. Complete the gaps with the missing words.

**Photograph 1**

1 It's not summer, _____ _____ .
2 This place is the _____ Dome. It's in _____ .

**Photograph 2**

3 The snow's _____ , but _____ it's a hot summer's day.
4 This is a photograph of the _____ Centre near _____ .

**Photograph 3**

5 It's _____ and there's _____ and there are rocks.
6 This is in Nebraska in the _____ _____ .

**8** Write the words from the box in the gaps.

> hot   inside   man-made   winter

1 In fact, it's not summer – it's _____ .
2 They're not natural. They're _____ .
3 The snow's _____ , but outside it's a _____ summer's day.

**9** 🔊 2.2 Listen again and check your answers.

## DISCUSSION

**10** Work in groups.

1 Choose a photograph (a–c), but do not say which one.
2 Take turns to talk about your photograph. Use the phrases from the box below.
3 Listen to the other students and guess the photograph.

> Take a look at this photograph. What can we see?
>
> It's …                          This place is …
>
> It's a/an …                    There's a/the … / There are …

Henry Doorly Zoo,
Omaha, Nebraska, US

Snow Centre, Hemel
Hempstead, England

Seagaia Ocean Dome,
Miyazaki, Japan

**UNLOCK** LISTENING AND SPEAKING SKILLS 1

# ⊙ LANGUAGE DEVELOPMENT

## MONTHS AND SEASONS

1  🔊 **2.3** Listen and match the words for seasons (1–7) to the correct sentences (a–g).

| | |
|---|---|
| 1  spring | a  There's a lot of rain in _____ in Thailand. |
| 2  summer | |
| 3  autumn | b  Russia gets a lot of snow in _____ . |
| 4  winter | c  _____ in Brazil begins in May. |
| 5  the dry season | d  _____ in England is from March to May. |
| 6  the rainy season | e  In _____ , the trees change colour from green to orange or red in Japan. |
| 7  the monsoon season | f  In Australia, _____ begins in December and ends in February. |
| | g  _____ in Nigeria is from March to October. |

2  Underline the words for months in sentences a–g in Exercise 1. Then write the months in the gaps.

1  January ☐       5  _____ ☐       9  September ☐
2  _____ ☐     6  June ☐            10  _____ ☐
3  _____ ☐     7  July ☐            11  November ☐
4  April ☐         8  August ☐          12  _____ ☐

3  🔊 **2.4** Listen and write the number of syllables (1, 2 or 3) next to the words in Exercise 2. Underline the syllables with stress. Then listen again and repeat.

4  Answer the questions. Use the phrases from the box below.

1  How many seasons are there in your country?
2  When is each season?

---

There are _____ (number) seasons in _____ (country).

They are _____ (seasons).

In my country, _____ (season) is from _____ (month) to _____ (month).

---

## WEATHER

**5** Match the pictures to the words for weather.

| picture | noun | adjective |
|---------|------|-----------|
| | sun | sunny |
| | snow | snowy |
| | wind | windy |
| | rain | rainy |
| | cloud | cloudy |
| | storm | stormy |

**6** Circle the correct word.

1 I'm happy when it's *sun / sunny*.
2 There's a big, black *cloud / cloudy* in the sky.
3 I have an umbrella for when it's *rain / rainy*.
4 We get a lot of *storms / stormy* in April.
5 We like to fly kites when it's *wind / windy*.

## COLOURS

**7** Match the words from the box to the correct colour.

> red   blue   yellow
> green   black   white
> orange

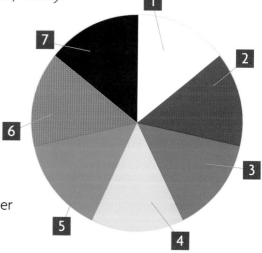

**8** Work with a partner. Ask and answer the questions from the box about the words and phrases below.

> What colour is ... ?   It's ... / It can be ... or ...
> What colour are ... ?   They're ... / They can be ... or ...

1 tomatoes
2 snow
3 trees
4 sand
5 clouds
6 your family's car

# LISTENING 2

## PREPARING TO LISTEN

**1** You are going to listen to two students describe a landscape. Look at the photographs of landscapes (a–e) and answer the questions.

USING VISUALS TO PREDICT CONTENT

   **1** What season is it in each photograph?

   **2** Describe the weather.

   **3** What colours can you see?

**2** Match the words from the box to the labels (1–7).

> desert   forest   island
> mountains   sea   sky   town

## WHILE LISTENING

UNL◯CK
ONLINE

**3** ◀)) **2.5** Listen to two students, Daniela and Altan, describe a landscape.

LISTENING FOR MAIN IDEAS

   **1** Write 'D' next to the photograph (a–c) Daniela describes.

   **2** Write 'A' next to the photograph (a–c) Altan describes.

   **3** Which photograph do they not describe?

**4** 🔊 **2.5** Listen again and circle the correct answers.

1 Daniela describes a landscape
   a in *spring / summer*.
   b in *Italy / Turkey*.
   c with a *park / beach*.
   d she thinks is *beautiful / ugly*.

2 Altan describes a landscape
   a in *his / another* country.
   b in *autumn / winter*.
   c with a famous *park / forest*.
   d on a *hot / cold* day.

## DISCUSSION

**5** Find a photograph of a place in your country or another country you know and answer the questions.

   1 Where is it?
   2 What season is it?
   3 Is the weather good?
   4 What can you see there?

**6** Work with a partner. Take turns to ask and answer the questions in Exercise 5 about your partner's photograph. Use the phrases from the box.

---

1 It's in _____ (*country*).

2 It's in _____ (*season*).

3 Yes/No , it's _____ (*weather adjective*).

4 You can see _____ (*place*).

   There's a _____ (*noun*).

   There are _____ (*noun*).

---

# CRITICAL THINKING

At the end of this unit, you are going to do the speaking task below.

> Describe photographs of a landscape.

**1** Work with a partner. Look at the photograph on pages 32–33 (Unlock your knowledge). Answer questions 1–5 in the table below.
Write 'Y' for *Yes* or 'N' for *No* in column 2.

UNDERSTAND

| questions | Y/N |
|---|---|
| 1 Is the photograph of a landscape? | |
| 2 Is the photograph of a place in your country? | |
| 3 Are there a lot of different colours in the photograph? | |
| 4 Is the photograph interesting? | |
| 5 Do you know key vocabulary to talk about this photograph? | |

**2** Work with a partner. Take turns to ask and answer questions about the photographs in Listening 1 (page 37) and Listening 2 (page 41).

## Choose visuals for a talk

Choose visuals that

- are interesting.
- show examples of key vocabulary.

**3** You are going to use the internet to find photographs of a landscape.

APPLY

1 Choose a natural place.
   beach ☐  desert ☐  forest ☐  island ☐  mountain ☐

2 Choose a season.
   spring ☐  summer ☐  autumn ☐  winter ☐  dry season ☐
   rainy season ☐  monsoon season ☐

3 Choose a kind of weather.
   cloud ☐  rain ☐  snow ☐  storm ☐  sun ☐  wind ☐

4 Choose a country you would like to visit.

**4** Use your words from Exercise 3 in an internet search. Find interesting photographs of a landscape.

# SPEAKING

## PREPARATION FOR SPEAKING

**1** 🔊 **2.6** Listen and match phrases 1–7 to sentences a–g.

| | |
|---|---|
| 1 I'm going to talk about | a _____ good morning, everybody. |
| 2 another photograph of | b OK, so _____ two photographs of a place in spring. |
| 3 I'm | c OK, so here's _____ . |
| 4 Here's | d Hello, everybody! OK, so, _____ Altan. |
| 5 OK, so, | e _____ Samsun. Samsun is in Turkey. |
| 6 I'm from | f _____ my first photograph. |
| 7 my first photograph | g Here's _____ the park. |

## PRONUNCIATION FOR SPEAKING

**2** 🔊 **2.6** Listen again. Underline the words with stress.

**3** 🔊 **2.6** Listen again and repeat. Say the underlined words louder.

**4** Look at the photographs. What can you see?

**5** 🔊 **2.7** Listen to a student describe the photographs. Then match the pairs.

1 Hello, everybody! ☐
2 OK, so today ☐
3 Here's my first photograph. ☐
4 OK, so where is this place? ☐
5 Here's another photograph of the mountain. ☐
6 It's a beautiful place. ☐

a It's in Japan. This is Mount Fuji.
b There's a path and you can see there are people there. There are a lot of white clouds below.
c I'm going to talk about two photographs of a place in spring.
d I want to go there.
e You can see there's a big mountain. There's a lot of snow. And there are trees. The trees are green and pink.
f OK, so I'm Khaled. I'm from Port Said.

**UNLOCK** LISTENING AND SPEAKING SKILLS 1

**6** Work with a partner. Take turns to describe the photographs in Exercise 4.

   1 Cover the text in Exercise 5.
   2 Make Khaled's talk true for you.

Hello everybody! OK, so, I'm ~~Khaled~~ Asya.
I'm from ~~Port Said~~ Izmir.

## THERE IS ... / THERE ARE ...

**7** Read Khaled's talk in Exercise 5. Underline the examples of

   1 *There's* (+ *a lot of*) + noun.
   2 *There's a* (+ adjective) + noun.
   3 *There are* (+ *a lot of*) + noun.

**8** 🔊 **2.8** Listen to Daniela and Altan. Write the words from the box in the gaps below.

> a lot of    forest    mountain    park    trees

   1 There's a _____ .
   2 There's a nice _____ .
   3 And there are _____ here.
   4 You can see there's a _____ in the photograph.
   5 You can see there are _____ white buildings.

EXPLANATION

Use *There is ...* (*There's ...*) / *There are ...* to talk about things you can see.

> There's **sand**. There's **snow** outside.
> There's **a beautiful beach**. There's **a lot of** snow.
> There are **people** on the beach. There are **rocks**.

Add *no* or *not any* in the negative.

> There's **no** sand. / There isn't any sand.
> There are **no** people on the beach. / There aren't any people on the beach.

The verb is before *there a / there any* in questions.

> Is there a forest there?
> Is there any snow outside?
> Are there any people on the beach?

**9** Work with a partner. Choose one photograph (a–c) from page 37 (Listening 1). Don't say which! Ask and answer the questions about it.

| questions | answers |
|---|---|
| 1 Where is it? | 1 It's in … |
| 2 What season is it? | 2 It's in … |
| 3 Are there any … in your photographs? | 3 Yes, there are some …<br>No, there aren't any … |
| 4 Is there a … in your photographs? | 4 Yes, there's a …<br>No, there isn't a … |

**10** Complete the gaps below with the phrases from the box. Use the nouns to help you.

> There's a    There's    There are

1 _____ **river** in the photograph.
2 _____ **snow** on the mountains.
3 _____ **people** on the beach.
4 _____ **trees** in the garden.
5 _____ small **town** in the mountains.
6 _____ red **car** in the desert.
7 _____ black **clouds** in the sky.

**11** 🔊 2.9 Listen and check your answers. Then listen again and repeat.

**12** Correct the mistakes in the sentences.

 1 There are a park.
 2 This are a mountain in the photograph.
 3 There's a cars by the houses.
 4 They's a big tree there.
 5 There snow on the mountains.

## ADJECTIVES

**13** Put the words and phrases in order to make sentences.

 1 black / are / The / clouds / .
 2 red and yellow / The / trees / are / .
 3 windy day / 's / a / It / .
 4 famous place / in / a / It / Thailand / 's / .
 5 small islands / are / in the / There / sea / .
 6 white mountain / 's / photograph / a / in the / There / .
 7 big house / 's / park / in / the / a/ You / can see / there / .
 8 young people / path / there / can see / You / are / on the / .

Use adjectives to describe age (*young, old*), size (*big, small*), nationality (*Turkish, Saudi*), colour (*red, green*) and quality (*hot, cold*).

Adjectives go after the verb *be* (*am/is/are*) or before a noun.

I'm Turkish. He's cold. It's windy.
I'm an English teacher. It's a sunny day.
There are white clouds in the sky.

We often stress adjectives.

**14** Correct the mistakes in the sentences.

1  It's sun in the photograph.
2  There's a windy.
3  There's a mountain big.

4  The people happy.
5  There's be a big forest.
6  It's a rain day.

**15** Work with a partner. Choose a photograph (a–c) from page 41 (Listening 2). Describe the photograph. Use the phrases from the box.

> This is a photograph of ...    You can see ...    It's a ... day.
> There's ... / There's a ... / There are ...

## SPEAKING TASK

**1** Use an internet search to find two photographs of a landscape. Search for

1  a country you would like to visit.
2  a place (e.g. a desert, a forest, an island).
3  a season (e.g. summer, winter, the monsoon season).
4  a kind of weather (e.g. snow, sun, rain).

PREPARE

**2** Choose two good photographs. Use questions 1–5 in Critical thinking Exercise 1 to help you (page 43).

**3** Find key vocabulary for your photographs.

**4** Write words in the gaps that are true for you and your photographs.

Hello everybody! I'm _____ (*your name*). I'm from _____ (*your town*). _____ (*your town*) is in _____ (*your country*). OK, so, I'm going to talk about two photographs of a place in _____ (*season*). Here's my first photograph.
[*Add descriptions using language you have seen in this unit.*]
Here's another photograph of _____ (*place*) in _____ (*season*). Where is this place? It's in _____ (*country*).
[*Add questions that you can ask the audience using language you have seen in this unit.*]

**5** Underline the words with stress in Exercise 4. Then practise your sentences with a partner.

**6** Work in groups.

1 Take turns to describe photographs or pictures of a favourite place.
2 Listen to the students in your group. Makes notes in the table.

|  | example | student 1 | student 2 |
|---|---|---|---|
| student's name | Khaled |  |  |
| country | Japan |  |  |
| place | mountain |  |  |
| season | spring |  |  |
| weather | sunny |  |  |
| things in the photographs | mountain, trees, clouds, path, people |  |  |

| TASK CHECKLIST | ✔ |
|---|---|
| Did you describe photographs of a landscape? |  |
| Did you choose words for an internet search? |  |
| Did you find key vocabulary for the photographs? |  |
| Did you use stress correctly in sentences? |  |

## OBJECTIVES REVIEW

*I can …*

understand a video about weather.

very well                                        not very well

use visuals to predict content.

very well                                        not very well

use phrases with *there is / there are.*

very well                                        not very well

use adjectives.

very well                                        not very well

describe photographs of a landscape.

very well                                        not very well

## WORDLIST

| UNIT VOCABULARY | |
| --- | --- |
| beautiful (adj) | path (n) |
| blue (adj) | sand (n) |
| cloud (n) | sea (n) |
| cold (adj) | see (v) |
| desert (n) | sky (n) |
| forest (n) | snow (n) |
| happy (adj) | summer (n) |
| hot (adj) | town (n) |
| inside (adj) | tree (n) |
| interesting (adj) | ugly (adj) |
| island (n) | unusual (adj) |
| man-made (adj) | wind (n) |
| natural (adj) | winter (n) |
| outside (adj) | |

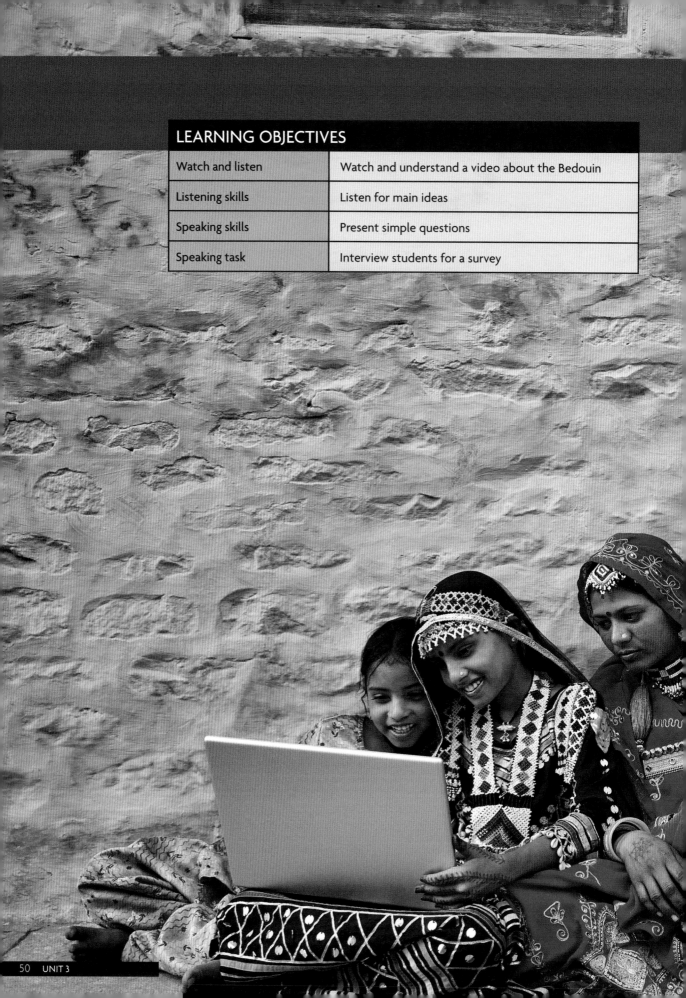

## LEARNING OBJECTIVES

| | |
|---|---|
| Watch and listen | Watch and understand a video about the Bedouin |
| Listening skills | Listen for main ideas |
| Speaking skills | Present simple questions |
| Speaking task | Interview students for a survey |

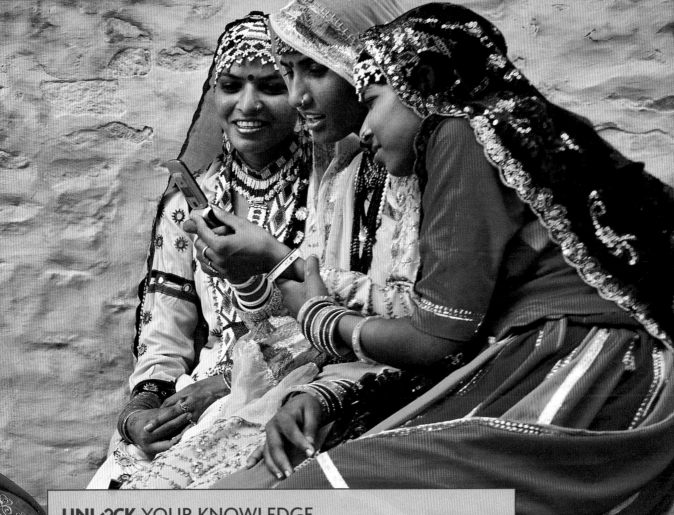

# LIFESTYLE   UNIT 3

## UNL⌀CK YOUR KNOWLEDGE

1 What can you see in the photograph?

2 Circle the phrases that are true for you.
- have a busy lifestyle
- use the internet or a mobile phone every day
- have a laptop or tablet
- like studying outside
- like studying with friends

3 Interview students in your class. Ask questions with *Do you ...?* about the phrases above. Discuss the answers with the rest of the class.

Do you have a busy lifestyle?

Do you use the internet every day?

# WATCH AND LISTEN

## PREPARING TO WATCH

**1** You are going to watch a video about the Bedouin. Before you watch, match an adjective from the box to the correct group of phrases below (1–6). Use each adjective only once.

> difficult   easy   happy   important   safe   traditional

**1** _____
- have a [...] lifestyle
- take [...] medicine
- 'Would you like to try some [...] Turkish cheese?'

**2** _____
- be [...] to eat
- be [...] to cross the road
- 'Have a [...] journey!'

**3** _____
- be [...] with somebody/ something
- feel [...]
- 'I'd be [...] to help you.'

**4** _____
- have a [...] problem
- be [...] to do something
- 'Some words are [...] to pronounce.'

**5** _____
- be [...] to do something
- be [...] to talk to
- 'This exercise is very [...]!'

**6** _____
- be an [...] person
- go on an [...] journey
- 'I have something [...] to tell you.'

**2** Write the adjectives from Exercise 1 in the gaps.

1 _____ medicine is very popular in China. Many people like it more than modern medicine.
2 This computer's very _____ to use. My children use it all the time.
3 My father is a manager at a hospital. He has a very _____ job.
4 Is this fish _____ to eat?
5 Can you help me? This question is _____ to answer.
6 I like my new phone. I'm really _____ with it.

**3** Look at the photographs from the video and answer the questions.

1 Where do the Bedouin live?
2 What animal can you see?
3 Is their life traditional or modern?

## WHILE WATCHING

**4** ▶ Watch the video. Circle the correct answers.

1 The Bedouin in this video are from
   a Sudan.
   b Saudi Arabia.
   c Egypt.
2 The old man is a Bedouin
   a doctor.
   b teacher.
   c taxi driver.
3 The children in the video are the old man's
   a grandchildren.
   b students.
   c customers.

**5** ▶ Watch again. Are the statements true (T) or false (F)?

1 The Bedouin lifestyle is not easy.            _____
2 Camels are important to the Bedouin lifestyle.  _____
3 The old man buys medicine from Cairo.         _____
4 The old man has four students.                _____
5 The boys are going to travel 160 kilometres.  _____
6 The old man is not happy with the boys.       _____

## DISCUSSION

**6** Work with a partner. Ask and answer the questions.

1 Are traditional lifestyles important?
2 Would you like to live a modern or a traditional lifestyle?

## PREPARING TO LISTEN

**1** You are going to listen to three conversations in different places. Before you listen, work with a partner. Ask and answer the questions in the table. Write 'Y' (yes) or 'N' (no).

| questions | you | your partner |
|---|---|---|
| 1 Do you <u>go to a gym</u>? | | |
| 2 Do you <u>do exercise</u> every day? | | |
| 3 Do you <u>smoke</u>? | | |
| 4 Do you <u>eat a lot of chocolate biscuits</u>? | | |

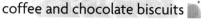
coffee and chocolate biscuits

doing exercise in a gym

**2** Are the underlined phrases in the table healthy or unhealthy?

### Intonation

Intonation is the way our voice goes up and down when we speak.

What's your name? ↘          Jennifer. ↘
Are you from New York? ↗     No. ↘ I'm from London. ↘

## PRONUNCIATION FOR LISTENING

**3** 🔊 **3.1** Listen to the dialogue from the explanation box and repeat.

**4** Circle the correct answers.

The voice
1 goes *up / down* in a *wh-* question.
2 goes *up / down* in a statement.
3 goes *up / down* in a 'Yes/No' question.

5 🔊 **3.2** Look at 1–6. Will the voice go up or down? Write ↗ or ↘ in the boxes. Then listen and check.

1 Can you tell me about the video? ☐
2 What's the problem? ☐
3 That's a good question. ☐
4 Do you need money for the gym? ☐
5 I like to be healthy. ☐
6 The university has a gym. ☐

## WHILE LISTENING

### Listening for main ideas

If you listen for the main idea(s), you try to understand these questions:

• Where are the speakers? (e.g. a university, a hospital, a hotel)
• Who are the speakers? (e.g. family, friends, teacher and students)
• Why are they speaking? (e.g. They need information, they want help, they want to teach something.)

6 🔊 **3.3** Listen to three conversations in different places. Write A, B or C next to the correct answer.

1 Which conversation is
 • in a café? _____
 • in a lecture? _____
 • on the phone? _____
2 Which conversation is between
 • a lecturer and a student? _____
 • a son and his father? _____
 • two students in the same class? _____
3 Which conversation has somebody that wants to ask
 • for information about a video? _____
 • somebody for money? _____
 • for information about lifestyle? _____

LISTENING FOR
MAIN IDEAS

UNL⌀CK
ONLINE

7 🔊 **3.3** Listen again and answer the questions.

In conversation A,
1 where does the son do exercise now?
2 why does he need money?

In conversation B,
3 which country does the student ask about?

In conversation C,
4 what is the video about?

LISTENING FOR
DETAIL

## DISCUSSION

**8** Work with a partner. Ask and answer the questions.

1 Do you live with your parents?
2 Would you like to live on your own?
3 Do you go to lectures?
4 Do students usually ask questions after a lecture?

# ⊙ LANGUAGE DEVELOPMENT

## DAYS OF THE WEEK

**1** 🔊 **3.4** Listen to the words for days of the week. Write the number of syllables next to the words (2 or 3).

Saturday ☐   Wednesday ☐   Friday ☐   Tuesday ☐
Sunday ☐   Thursday ☐   Monday ☐

**2** Which days

1 do you go to school/university?
2 are the weekend in your country?
3 do you have your English class?
4 do you spend time with your friends and family?

## TIME EXPRESSIONS

**3** Read the sentences below. Underline

- the times.
- the parts of the day.
- the days.

1 Fahd has breakfast at <u>6.30</u> in the <u>morning</u>.
2 Chen and Wang watch films every Tuesday evening.
3 My sister makes my lunch on Wednesdays.
4 I play football with my friends every Saturday.
5 Faisal goes home at 3.00 in the afternoon.
6 Tania gets up at 6.00 in the morning.
7 Abdullah has English class at 7.30 in the evening.
8 Fatima has coffee with her friends every day.
9 Hakan goes to work at 8.30 in the morning.
10 Kerry has dinner at 6.30 in the evening.

**4** Look at the sentences in Exercise 3 again. Then write the words from the box in the gaps below.

> every   in   on   at

1 ____every____ + noun (e.g. *day, Saturday, Tuesday evening*)
2 _____ the morning / the afternoon / the evening
3 _____ + clock time (e.g. *7.30*)
4 _____ + day of the week (e.g. *Tuesday*)

**5** Read this text about a student. Write *in, on* or *at* in the gaps.

This is Élodie. She's from France. She takes the bus to university every day. The bus comes (1)_____ 7.30. Élodie arrives (2)_____ 8.30. She has a biology lecture (3)_____ nine (4)_____ Tuesday and Thursday. She has lunch with her friends (5)_____ 12.30. Elodie has an English class (6)_____ three o'clock (7)_____ the afternoon. She goes to the cinema with her family (8)_____ Friday evening.

**6** 🔊 **3.5** Listen and check.

## THE PRESENT SIMPLE

**7** Work with a partner. Take turns to close your book and answer the questions about Élodie.

1 Where's she from?
2 Where does she go every day?
3 What time does the bus come?
4 Does she have a maths lecture on Tuesday morning?
5 When does she have English class?
6 What does she do on Friday evening?

**8** Write the verbs from the box in the gaps. Look at the verbs in Exercises 3, 5 and 7 to help you.

get   go   have   make   play   take   watch

1 _____ breakfast / lunch / dinner / coffee / a lesson / a lecture
2 _____ films / TV
3 _____ breakfast / lunch / dinner / coffee
4 _____ football / basketball / tennis / computer games
5 _____ home / to work / to university
6 _____ up (in the morning)
7 _____ a bus / a taxi / a train

## The present simple

Use the present simple to talk about regular activities. Add -s or -es to the verb after *he/she/it*.

> I play tennis every week. You study English. We go home early on Tuesday. They study biology.
> She takes the bus. He goes to work early. It makes good coffee.

Use *do not* + verb or *does not* + verb in the negative.

> I don't watch films. We don't go home early today. (*don't = do not*)
> She doesn't take the bus. He doesn't go to work early. (*doesn't = does not*)

Use *do* or *does* + subject + verb in questions.

> Do you have dinner at home? Where does she go every day?

NB The verb *have* is irregular. Use *has* with *he/she/it*.

> ~~He haves a good car~~. He has a good car.

**9** Work with a partner. Use the phrases from Exercise 8 to ask questions.

> When <u>do you have</u> breakfast?
> <u>Do you play</u> football?
> When <u>do you get</u> up?
> <u>Do you take</u> a bus to school?

**10** Work with a new partner. Tell him/her about your partner from Exercise 9.

> She <u>has</u> breakfast at seven.
> She <u>doesn't play</u> football.
> She <u>gets up</u> early.
> She <u>doesn't take</u> a bus to school.

# LISTENING 2

## PREPARING TO LISTEN

**1** 🔊 **3.6** You are going to listen to an interview. Before you hear it, listen to these dialogues and circle the phrases you hear.

UNDERSTANDING KEY VOCABULARY

1  **A:** Excuse me! Can I ask you some questions?
   **B:** *Yes, no problem. / I don't have time, I'm sorry.*

2  **A:** I'd like to ask some questions – is that OK?
   **B:** *Yes, sure. / I'm sorry, I'm very busy.*

3  **A:** Good morning! I'm Sultan.
   **B:** *Nice to meet you! / Good to see you!* I'm Jack.

4  **A:** Do you drink a lot of coffee?
   **B:** *Yes, I think so / No, not really.*

5  **A:** I play football for my country.
   **B:** *Really? / I see.*

6  **A:** I watch a lot of films.
   **B:** *Really? / I see.*

**2** Work with a partner. Practise the dialogues.

## WHILE LISTENING

**3** 🔊 **3.7** Listen to an interview and answer the questions.

LISTENING FOR MAIN IDEAS

1  Where are the speakers?
   **a** in a university
   **b** in a café
   **c** in the street

2  Who are the speakers?
   **a** two strangers
   **b** a teacher and a student
   **c** good friends

3  What does one of the speakers want information about?
   **a** lifestyles
   **b** journeys
   **c** gyms

**4** 🔊 **3.7** Listen again. Write Jasvinder's answers in the questionnaire.

# QUESTIONNAIRE

**Name:** Jasvinder    **Job:** university student

**A Home/Family**

A1   Do you live with your parents?   Y ◯   N ◯

**B Work/Studies**

B1   Do you work or study?    work ◯   study ◯

B2   What's your job? / What do you study?   biology

**C Lifestyle**

C1   Do you have a busy lifestyle?   Y ◯   N ◯

C2a   How do you relax?

C2b   Do you like exercise?    Y ◯   N ◯

C2c   Do you go to a gym?    Y ◯   N ◯

C2d   Do you go to the cinema?    Y ◯   N ◯

C3a   When do you go out with friends?

C3b   Where do you go with your friends?

## PRACTICE

**5** Work with a partner. Use the questionnaire to role-play an interview. Use the phrases from the boxes.

**Asking**
- Excuse me! Can I ask you some questions?
- I'm … . What's your name?
- I'm … .
- Nice to meet you!
- OK, do you … ?

**Answering**
- Yes, sure. / Yes, no problem.
- Yes. / Yes, I think so.
- No. / No, not really.

**6** Work with a new partner. Use the questionnaire to tell your new partner about the student in Exercise 5.

# CRITICAL THINKING

At the end of this unit, you are going to do the speaking task below.

Interview students for a survey.

## Use surveys

In a survey, you use a questionnaire to find out information. For example, you can ask questions to learn about the lifestyles of students in your school or university.

1 Before you write a survey think of topics (a–d) and questions you can ask about each topic, using the ideas map below.

CREATE

Do you watch films at the cinema?

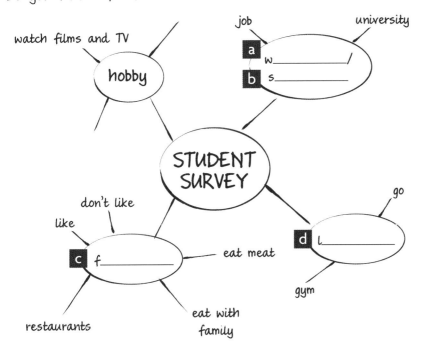

2 Put the help for how to do a survey in the correct order.

REMEMBER

☐ Record the answers.
☐ Write questions.
☐ Practise saying the questions.
☐ Be polite when you ask the questions.
☐ Choose a topic.

## PREPARATION FOR SPEAKING

### COLLOCATIONS FOR LIFESTYLE

> **Collocations**
>
> A collocation is a group of words. A collocation can be:
> - a verb + noun / noun phrase: *download apps, write a blog*
> - a verb + preposition phrase: *go to a gym, eat at home*
> - a verb + adverb: *chat online*

**1** Write the verbs from the box in the gaps (1–9) in the table below.

> cook   do   download   eat   go   order   ~~post~~   watch   write

**2** Write the topics from the box at the top of the correct column (a–c).

> food   free time   technology

| (a) _____ | (b) _____ | (c) _____ |
|---|---|---|
| • **send** texts/ photographs <br> • (1) _post_ a video online <br> • **chat** online <br> • (2) _____ apps <br> • **follow** a blog <br> • (3) _____ a blog | • (4) _____ food for your family <br> • **eat** out at restaurants <br> • **have** coffee with friends <br> • (5) _____ at home <br> • **have** dinner with friends <br> • (6) _____ fast food | • **go out** with friends <br> • (7) _____ TV <br> • **go** to the cinema <br> • (8) _____ sport and exercise <br> • **play** computer games <br> • (9) _____ to the gym |

**UNLOCK** LISTENING AND SPEAKING SKILLS 1

## PRESENT SIMPLE QUESTIONS

**3** Put the words in the correct order to make questions.

1 in / the / Do / watch / TV / evening / you / ?
2 cook / Do / for / family / you / food / your / ?
3 restaurants / eat / you / out / at / Do / ?
4 you / blog / write / a / Do / ?
5 do / computer / Which / games / play / you / ?
6 every / many / do / texts / send / day / How / you / ?

**4** ◀)**3.8** Match a question from Exercise 3 (1–6) to the answers (a–f). Then listen and check.

a No, but I follow one. It's about football.
b No, not really. I go to the gym in the evening.
c I'm not sure. I send a lot of them – 40 or 50, maybe?
d No! I can order pizza but I can't cook!
e I like *NBA Basketball*. I play it on my PC.
f Yes. I go with my family every Monday evening.

**5** Work with a partner. Role-play the dialogues from Exercise 4.

**6** Work with a new partner. Ask and answer the questions in Exercise 3.

**7** Correct the mistakes in the questions.

1 For your family, you cook food?
2 You eat out at restaurants?
3 Are you have coffee with friends?
4 What you eat at home?
5 Where have you dinner with friends?
6 What kind fast food do you like?

**8** Match the *wh-* questions (1–6) to the answers (a–f).

1 Where do you go with your friends?
2 What do you study?
3 Who are the speakers?
4 Why are they speaking?
5 Which bus do you take to school?
6 When do you go out with your friends?

a Biology
b Friends
c The number 3
d To a café
e On Saturday
f They need information.

## PRONUNCIATION FOR SPEAKING

**9** 🔊 **3.9** Listen and repeat.

1 What food do you like? ☐
2 Do you watch the news? ☐
3 Do you read books? ☐
4 What football team do you like? ☐
5 Do you cook dinner in the evening? ☐
6 Which bus do you take to school? ☐

**10** 🔊 **3.9** Listen again and answer the questions.

1 Does the voice go up or down in these questions? Write ↘ or ↗ in each box.
2 How do we pronounce *do you*?

**11** 🔊 **3.10** Listen and repeat.

| /uː/ | /ʊ/ |
|---|---|
| true | good |
| room | would |
| computer | pull |

**12** 🔊 **3.11** Listen to these words from the questions in Exercise 9. Write them in the correct column of the table above.

food    you    news    books
football    cook    school

**13** Work with a partner. Ask and answer the questions in Exercise 9. Write or record your interviews.

**14** Write six questions with the collocations for *food* in Exercises 1 and 2. Write three *Do you ...?* and three *Wh- ...?* questions.

**15** Practise saying the questions.

**16** Work with a partner. Take turns to ask and answer the questions.

**UNLOCK** LISTENING AND SPEAKING SKILLS 1

## SPEAKING TASK

**1** Work in two groups: A and B.

### Group A
Write six questions with the collocations for *technology* in Exercises 1 and 2 on page 62. Write three *Do you* ... ? and three *Wh-* ...? questions in the survey below.

### Group B
Write six questions with the collocations for *free time* in Exercises 1 and 2 on page 62. Write three *Do you* ... ? and three *Wh-* ...? questions in the survey below.

# QUESTIONNAIRE

| | Name: Student 1 | Name: Student 2 | Name: Student 3 |
|---|---|---|---|
| **A  Technology** | | | |
| A1 _____ | _____ | _____ | _____ |
| A2 _____ | _____ | _____ | _____ |
| A3 _____ | _____ | _____ | _____ |
| A4 _____ | _____ | _____ | _____ |
| A5 _____ | _____ | _____ | _____ |
| A6 _____ | _____ | _____ | _____ |
| **B  Free time** | | | |
| B1 _____ | _____ | _____ | _____ |
| B2 _____ | _____ | _____ | _____ |
| B3 _____ | _____ | _____ | _____ |
| B4 _____ | _____ | _____ | _____ |
| B5 _____ | _____ | _____ | _____ |
| B6 _____ | _____ | _____ | _____ |

**2** Interview three students from the other group. Remember to write or record the answers to the questions.

**3** Share the answers to your questions with your group. Remember to add *-s* to the verbs!

Asya **downloads** apps for Android. Natsuko **downloads** apps for Apple.
Chen **goes out** with friends on Saturday. Fahd **plays** football on Tuesday and Thursday.

**4** Work with a partner from the other group. Tell your partner about the answers to your group's questions.

| TASK CHECKLIST | ✔ |
|---|---|
| Did you interview students for a survey? | |
| Did you use the present simple to write questions? | |
| Did you use the correct intonation? | |

## OBJECTIVES REVIEW

*I can ...*

understand a video about the Bedouin.

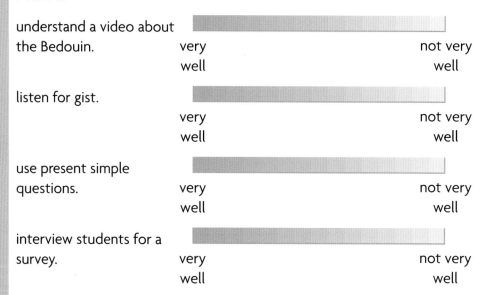

very well           not very well

listen for gist.

very well           not very well

use present simple questions.

very well           not very well

interview students for a survey.

very well           not very well

# WORDLIST

| UNIT VOCABULARY | |
| --- | --- |
| app (n) | intonation (n) |
| biscuit (n) | laptop (n) |
| blog (n) | lifestyle (n) |
| busy (adj) | online (adj) |
| chat (v) | polite (adj) |
| chocolate (n) | post (v) |
| down (prep) | practise (v) |
| download (v) | record (v) |
| eat (v) | send (v) |
| exercise (n) | smoke (v) |
| follow (v) | survey (n) |
| go out (v) | up (prep) |
| gym (n) | use (v) |
| healthy (adj) | write (v) |
| important (adj) | |

## LEARNING OBJECTIVES

| Watch and listen | Watch and understand a video about a reef |
|---|---|
| Listening skills | Listen for detail |
| Speaking skills | Ask for and give directions; the imperative |
| Speaking task | Ask for and give directions |

## UNL⌀CK YOUR KNOWLEDGE

Work with a partner. Ask and answer the questions.

1 What can you see in the photograph?
2 Have you been to a place like this?
3 Is it similar to somewhere in your country?

# WATCH AND LISTEN

 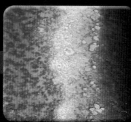   

## PREPARING TO WATCH

UNDERSTANDING
KEY VOCABULARY

**1** Write the words from the box in the sentences for each photograph.

> bright   coral   dangerous   famous   scuba diver
> shark   Tourists   underwater

Ahmed is a (1)_____ . He takes
(2)_____ photographs.

Many reef fish have
(3)_____ colours.

The 'flowers' in this photograph
are (4)_____ – a kind of
animal that lives on reefs.

(5)_____ travel all over the world.
They often go to (6)_____ places
and take a lot of photographs.

This is a (7)_____ . It is a very
(8)_____ animal.

**2** Work with a partner. Ask and answer questions about the key vocabulary in Exercise 1. Use the phrases from the box.

| | |
|---|---|
| What's a … (e.g. *shark*)? | It's a … |
| What's … (e.g. *coral*)? | It's … |
| What are … (e.g. *tourists*)? | They're … |

**3** Work with a partner. Predict the answers to the questions and circle the best answers. Use your own knowledge and ideas.

USING YOUR KNOWLEDGE TO PREDICT CONTENT

1 The reef is in
  a Italy.     b Australia.     c Mexico.
2 The reef is
  a not old.     b old.     c very old.
3 The reef is
  a small.     b big.     c very big.
4 The reef is popular with
  a fishermen.     b scientists.     c tourists.
5 Whales go to the reef in
  a winter.     b summer.     c spring.

## WHILE WATCHING

**4** ▶ Watch the video. Check your answers to the questions in Exercise 3.

UNDERSTANDING MAIN IDEAS

**5** ▶ Watch again. Match a number from the video (1–5) to the correct fact (a–e).

UNDERSTANDING DETAIL

1 1,600     a age of the reef in years
2 5,000,000,000     b number of islands on the reef
3 900     c different kinds of coral on the reef
4 10,000     d different kinds of fish on the reef
5 400     e money from tourism in dollars

## DISCUSSION

**6** Work with a partner. Ask and answer the questions.

Would you like to
- visit Australia?
- go scuba diving?
- see a shark/whale?
- swim underwater?

# LISTENING 1

## PREPARING TO LISTEN

PRONUNCIATION FOR LISTENING

**1** 🔊 **4.1** Listen and write the words you hear from the table in the gaps.

| | |
|---|---|
| this | that |
| these | those |
| here | there |

1 Where is _____ ?
2 What are _____ red circles?
3 The blue one _____ and the yellow one _____ .
4 Yes, _____'s a good example.
5 _____ cities have a lot of important places.
6 The economy is good _____ .

**2** 🔊 **4.1** Listen again.

1 Do the words from the table have stress?
2 Does the voice go up (↗) or down (↘) on these words?

EXPLANATION

### Stress in direction words

Stress the words

- *this*, *these* and *here* to point to things that are near.
- *that*, *those* and *there* to point to things that are not near.

UNDERSTANDING KEY VOCABULARY

**3** You are going to hear part of a geography seminar. Before you listen, write the words from the box in the vocabulary diagram below.

America  east  Europe  Holland  Istanbul  Italy  London
Madrid  Moscow  north  Paris  Rotterdam  south  Spain  west

**4** Work with a partner. Look at Map 1 and discuss the questions.

1 What region can you see in this map?

2 Do you know the names of the countries/cities (A–G)?

3 Which countries can you see on the blue line? Which countries can you see on the yellow line?

Map 1

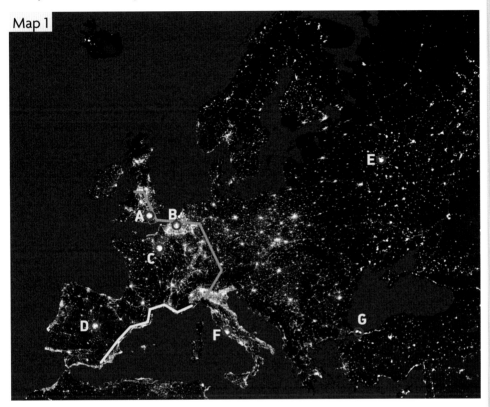

## WHILE LISTENING

**5** 🔊 **4.2** Listen to part of a geography seminar and choose the correct answers.

1 What does *mega* mean?

a  very important

b  very big

c  very bright

2 The lecturer says that the red circles on the map are

a  capital cities.

b  big cities.

c  important countries.

3 The seminar is about groups of

a  tourists.

b  capital cities.

c  big cities.

## Listening for detail

A detail is a fact about something. A detail can be

- a number, a letter, an address.

- a question or instruction.

- an example of something.

**6** 🔊 **4.2** Listen again. Are these statements true (T) or false (F)?

1 The map shows Europe in the day. _____

2 Paris is the city at 'C'. _____

3 The blue and yellow lines are roads. _____

4 Istanbul and Shanghai are examples of megaregions. _____

5 Megaregions are important for business. _____

6 The 'blue banana' is a place in Spain. _____

7 The city at 'B' has a good economy. _____

## DISCUSSION

**7** Work with a partner. Ask and answer the questions.

1 Do you live in an big city? (If not, would you like to live in a big city?)

2 Which cities are important in your country?

3 Is your city part of a megaregion? (If yes, what are the other cities in the region?)

# ⊙ LANGUAGE DEVELOPMENT

UNLOCK
ONLINE

## VOCABULARY FOR PLACES

**1** Use the words from the box to answer the questions below.

> bank   bridge   library   mosque   park
> port   station   supermarket

1 Where can you see a lot of ships?

2 Where can you pray?

3 Where can you find lots of books?

4 What goes over a river?

5 Where can you buy food?

6 Where can you put your money?

7 Where can you go for a walk?

8 Where can you take a train?

**2** 🔊 **4.3** Listen to eight short conversations. Write the words you hear in the gaps.

   1  Where's the _____ ? Is it near the bank?
   2  Is there a _____ near here?
   3  Where's the Blue _____ ? Is it in Cairo?
   4  Excuse me, where's the _____ ?
   5  I can't find the _____ – is it near here?
   6  Where's the _____ ?
   7  Where can I get a _____ ?
   8  I'm looking for the _____ . Is it near the bridge?

**The Blue Mosque in Istanbul**

**3** 🔊 **4.3** Listen again. Match each question from Exercise 2 (1–8) to an answer (a–h).

   a  Yes, it's between the bank and the bookshop.
   b  Yes. There's one next to the train station.
   c  No. It's there on the left. It's behind that school.
   d  At the bus stop over there. Can you see it?
   e  No. It's in the old town of Istanbul.
   f  It's opposite the restaurant on Tower Street.
   g  Yes, it's behind the bank.
   h  It's in front of that big clock. There – on the right.

## PREPOSITIONS OF PLACE

**4** Find these prepositions in a–h (Exercise 3) and circle them.

> at   behind   between   in   in front of
> next to   on   opposite

**5** Write the prepositions under the pictures.

> at    behind    between    in    in front of
> next to    on    opposite

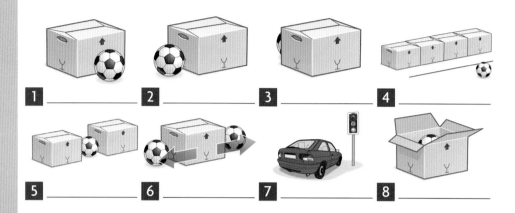

| 1 _____ | 2 _____ | 3 _____ | 4 _____ |
| 5 _____ | 6 _____ | 7 _____ | 8 _____ |

# LISTENING 2

## PREPARING TO LISTEN

USING YOUR KNOWLEDGE

**1** You are going to listen to some students take a quiz. Before you listen, look at Map 2. What kind of place can you see? Circle the correct answer.

a  a map of an international airport

b  a map of a university campus

c  a map of a small town

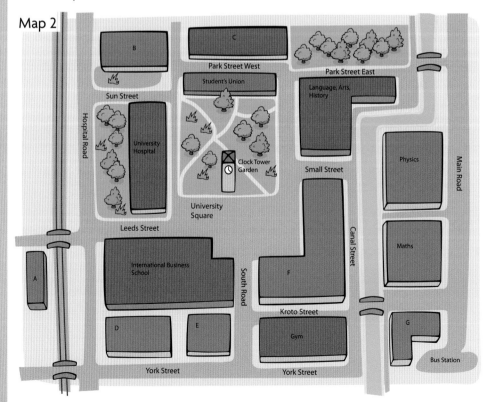

Map 2

**UNLØCK** LISTENING AND SPEAKING SKILLS 1

**2** Look at the map. Are the statements true (T) or false (F)?

1 There are three bridges on Hospital Road. _____

2 There are three buildings on York Street. _____

3 The Physics building is opposite the International Business School. _____

4 The Language, Arts and History building is between Small Street and York Street. _____

5 There's a Chemistry building on Main Road. _____

6 There's a small garden next to the hospital. _____

7 The Student's Union building is on Park Street West. _____

8 There is a bus station on Canal Street. _____

## WHILE LISTENING

**3** 🔊 **4.4** Listen to some students take a quiz and choose the correct answers.

LISTENING FOR MAIN IDEAS

**UNLOCK ONLINE**

1 The students are

   a in the Student's Union.

   b in front of the University Hospital.

   c at the clock.

2 How many teams take the quiz?

   a two   b three   c four

3 Who asks the questions?

   a the teacher

   b the students

   c the teacher and the students

**4** 🔊 **4.4** Listen again and answer the questions. Look at Map 2 and write A–G for the answers.

LISTENING FOR DETAIL

Where's the

1 train station? _____

2 Chemistry building? _____

3 supermarket? _____

4 library? _____

5 bank? _____

## PRACTICE

**5** Work with a partner. Look at Map 2 again. You are in the Student's Union building. Take turns to ask and answer the questions.

> **Where's the gym?**

> Can you tell me the way to the International Business School?

> **How do I get to the gym?**

> **Is there a bus station?**

## DISCUSSION

**6** Work with a partner. Look at the maps below, then ask and answer the questions.

1 Which kind of map can you see on page 76 (Listening 2)?
2 Which kind of map(s) do
  **a** scientists use?
  **b** people use to drive?
3 Which kind of map is best for tourists?

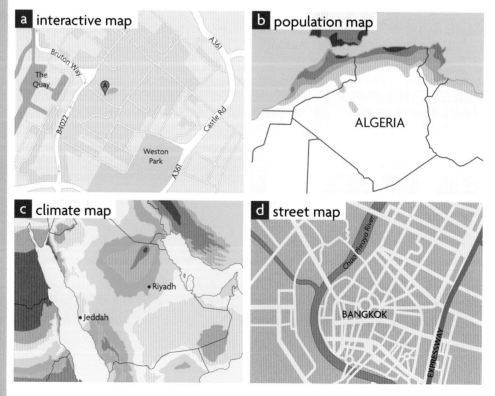

a interactive map

b population map

ALGERIA

c climate map

d street map

BANGKOK

**UNLOCK** LISTENING AND SPEAKING SKILLS 1

# CRITICAL THINKING

At the end of this unit, you are going to do the speaking task below.

Ask for and give directions.

## Giving directions

Use prepositions of place to make your directions clear.

UNDERSTAND

**1** Look at Map 3 and write the words from the box in the gaps below.

across along around down into out of
over through (turn) left/right up under

Map 3

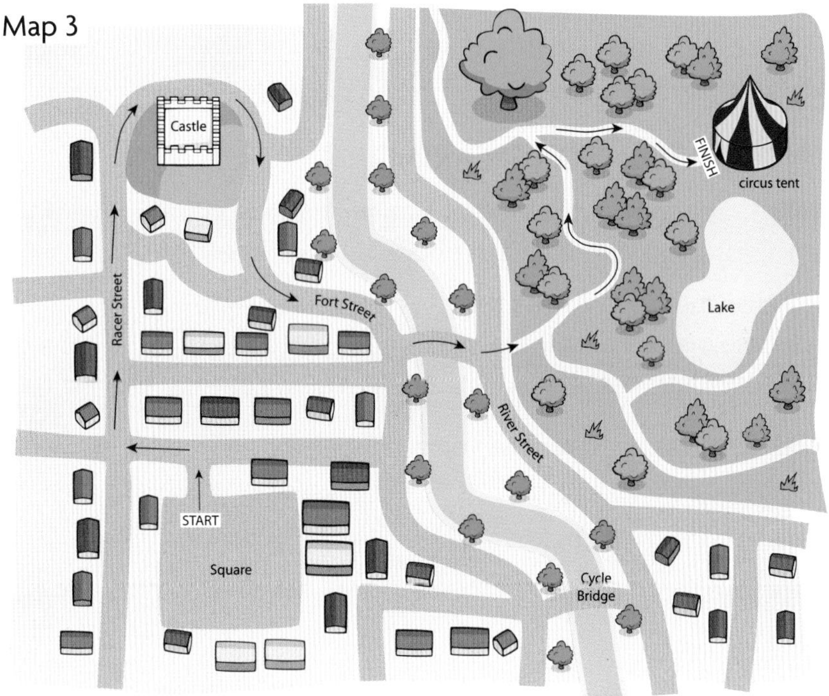


Go (1)__________ the square and turn (2)__________ . Go (3)__________ Racer Street and (4)__________ the hill to the castle. Go (5)__________ the castle and (6)__________ Fort Street to the river, and then go (7)__________ the bridge. Go (8)__________ the road and (9)__________ the park to a big tree. When you are (10)__________ the tree, turn (11)__________ and go (12)__________ the tent.

APPLY

**2** Work with a partner. Can you give different directions to go to the tent?

# SPEAKING

## PREPARATION FOR SPEAKING

### ASKING FOR DIRECTIONS

1 🔊 **4.5** Put the words in the correct order. Then listen and check.

1 's / the / Where / gym / ?
2 there / near / a / café / Is / here / ?
3 Language / do / Centre / to / the / I / How / get / ?
4 tell / way / station / me / Can / train / you / the / to / ?
5 looking / here / near / . / the / Is / library / for / I'm / it / ?

2 🔊 **4.6** Listen to three people ask for directions. Which question (1–5) from Exercise 1 do they ask?

a Excuse me! _____ , please?
b Excuse me! I think I'm lost. _____ ?
c Excuse me! _____ ?

## PRONUNCIATION FOR SPEAKING

3 🔊 **4.7** Listen to these questions. Underline the words or parts of words with stress. (You will hear each phrase by itself, then the whole question.)

1 Ex-cuse me!    Where's the        bank, please?
2 Ex-cuse me!    I think I'm lost.    How do I get to      the gym?
3 Ex-cuse me!    Can you tell me     the way to           the ca-fé?

4 🔊 **4.7** Listen again. Does the voice go up or down (➚ or ➘) in

1 the phrase *Excuse me!*?          3 the questions in 1 and 2?
2 the phrase *I think I'm lost*?     4 the question in 3?

5 🔊 **4.7** Listen again. Repeat each phrase you hear. Then repeat the whole question.

### Pronunciation of phrases

A statement or question has one or more phrases. A phrase has one or two stressed words. Practise your pronunciation phrase by phrase.

6 Work with a partner. Look at the map on page 76 (Listening 2).

Student A:  Listen to Student B. Point to the places he/she asks directions for.
Student B:  Choose four places on the map. Ask Student A for directions.

7 Change roles and do Exercise 6 again.

**UNL*CK** LISTENING AND SPEAKING SKILLS 1

# GIVING DIRECTIONS

**8** 🔊 **4.8** Listen and write the words from the box in the gaps below.

> along   at   behind   in   in   on   on
> opposite   over   through   to

1 It's _____ the International Business School.
2 It's _____ the old town of Istanbul.
3 Go _____ Clock Tower Garden **to** the Student's Union.
4 It's _____ **front of** that big clock. There – _____ **the right**.
5 OK then, so we're _____ the clock.
6 Go _____ Leeds Street. Then go _____ **the bridge**.
7 There's one **next** _____ the train station.
8 It's there _____ **the left**. It's _____ **that school**.

**9** Which sentences (1–8) in Exercise 8

a describe location?
b give directions?

**10** Look at the map on page 76 (Listening 2). Circle the correct words to give directions to the bank.

> It's (1) *behind / in front of* the International Business School. Go along Leeds Street and then turn (2) *left / right*. Go (3) *along / through* Hospital Road and turn (4) *left / right*. There are three buildings (5) *at / on* York Street. The bank is (6) *in front of / next to* the café and (7) *opposite / next to* the gym (8) *at / on* South Road.

## The imperative

Use the imperative to give instructions and directions. There is no pronoun in the imperative.

Go along South Road.          Go over the bridge.
Turn right at the bank.

# SPEAKING TASK

**PREPARE**

**1** You are going to help a group of new students at your university. Work in groups, A and B.

Group A:    Turn to page 194.
Group B:    Turn to page 196.

**PRACTISE**

**2** Work with a student from the other group.

Student A:    Look at the map on page 194. Give directions to Student B.
Student B:    Look at the map below. Ask Student A for directions to the places below (1–5). Write the correct letter (A–E) next to each place.

## The University of Alpha

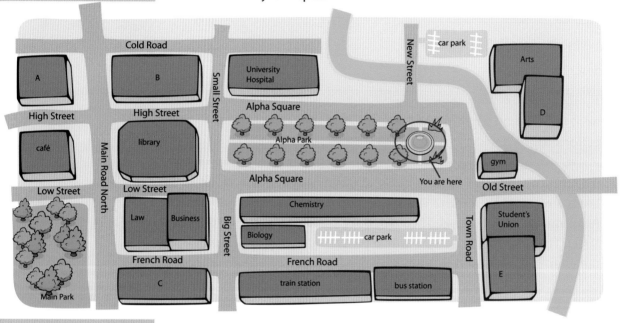

1  the History building     _____
2  the supermarket          _____
3  the bank                 _____
4  the Physics building     _____
5  the Language Centre       _____

**3** Change roles.

Student A:  Look at this new map. Ask Student B for directions to the places below (1–5). Write the correct letter (A–E) next to each place.

Student B:  Look at the map on page 196. Give directions to Student A.

## The University of Beta

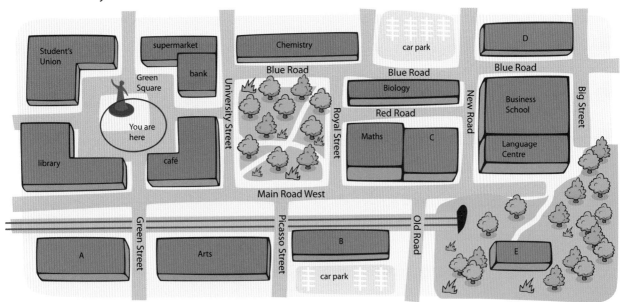

1  the gym _____
2  the Physics building _____
3  the train station _____
4  the bus station _____
5  the History building _____

**4** Use the maps on pages 194 and 196 to check your answers.

| TASK CHECKLIST | ✔ |
|---|---|
| Did you ask for directions? | |
| Did you give directions? | |
| Did you describe location (e.g. *behind*, *on*, *in*, etc.)? | |
| Did you practise your pronunciation of phrases? | |

## OBJECTIVES REVIEW

*I can ...*

understand a video about
a reef.

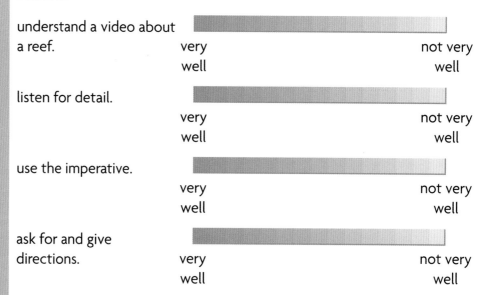

| very | not very |
|---|---|
| well | well |

listen for detail.

| very | not very |
|---|---|
| well | well |

use the imperative.

| very | not very |
|---|---|
| well | well |

ask for and give
directions.

| very | not very |
|---|---|
| well | well |

# WORDLIST

| UNIT VOCABULARY | |
| --- | --- |
| across (prep) | old (adj) |
| airport (n) | on (prep) |
| along (prep) | opposite (prep) |
| around (prep) | out of (prep) |
| at (prep) | over (prep) |
| bank (n) | park (n) |
| behind (prep) | political (n) |
| between (prep) | population (n) |
| bridge (n) | port (n) |
| bus station (n) | restaurant (n) |
| climate (n) | right (adj) |
| clock (n) | road (n) |
| east (n) | satellite (n) |
| garden (n) | school (n) |
| here (adv) | south (n) |
| hospital (n) | station (n) |
| hotel (n) | street (n) |
| in (prep) | supermarket (n) |
| in front of (prep) | that (det, pron) |
| into (prep) | there (adv) |
| left (adj) | these (det, pron) |
| library (n) | this (det, pron) |
| modern (adj) | those (det, pron) |
| mosque (n) | through (prep) |
| new (adj) | turn (v) |
| next to (adj) | under (adj) |
| north (n) | west (n) |

## LEARNING OBJECTIVES

| Watch and listen | Watch and understand a video about free diving |
|---|---|
| Listening skills | Use your knowledge of the topic to help you understand |
| Speaking skills | Make comparisons; sports collocations; introduce a talk |
| Speaking task | Compare different kinds of sport and exercise |

## UNLOCK YOUR KNOWLEDGE

Work with a partner. Ask and answer the questions.

1 What sport can you see in the photograph?
2 Do you have a favourite sport?
3 Do you like watching sport?

## PREPARING TO WATCH

**1** ▶ You are going to watch a video about free diving. Watch the video without sound. Write words for things you see in the table.

| people (e.g. *an old woman*) | places (e.g. *a school*) |
|---|---|
| | |
| **things (e.g. *a car*)** | **times of day (e.g. *afternoon*)** |
| | |

**2** Work with a partner. Compare your tables.

**3** Look at the table on page 198. How many words do you have? Circle the words that are the same.

**4** What is *free diving*? Circle the correct answer.

a diving under water to take photographs of fish
b diving under water to go fishing
c diving under water without equipment

# WHILE WATCHING

**5** ▶ Watch again with sound. Circle the correct answers.

1 How many people live in Sicily?
   a 3 **million**
   b 4 million
   c 5 million

2 Fishing in Sicily is a
   a big business.
   b **traditional** business.
   c modern business.

3 Why does Michaele Ralo go free diving every day?
   a Because he likes swimming in the sea.
   b Because he thinks **ancient** traditions are **important**.
   c Because he wants to be a **professional** free diver.

4 Why are scuba divers at the free-diving **competition**?
   a to help free divers that have a problem
   b to take photographs for **fans** of free diving
   c to watch the competition

5 How **deep** is Michaele Ralo's dive?
   a more than 40 metres
   b more than 50 metres
   c more than 60 metres

**6** Look at Exercise 5 again and use the words in bold to complete these sentences.

1 This swimming pool is three metres _deep_ .
2 The basketball players LeBron James and Kobe Bryant have a lot of _____ .
3 There are six zeros (000,000) in a _____ .
4 Today, a _____ footballer can make a lot of money.
5 The Olympics is an international sports _____ .
6 The Bedouin have a _____ lifestyle.
7 Ephesus is an _____ city in Turkey. It is more than 2,000 years old.
8 It is _____ to speak two or more languages.

# DISCUSSION

**7** Free diving is a dangerous sport. What other sports are dangerous? Make a list.

**8** Work with a partner. Ask and answer the questions about the dangerous sports in your lists.

1 Which sports are more dangerous than the others?
2 Would you like to do a dangerous sport? If yes, which one? Why?

## PREPARING TO LISTEN

UNDERSTANDING
KEY VOCABULARY

1 You are going to listen to a lecture about sport. Before you listen, look at the photographs and ask and answer the questions. Use the words from the box to help you.

> the back   a bone   a martial art   tae kwon do   yoga

1 What sport is in photograph A? What kind of sport is it?
2 What kind of exercise is in photograph B?
3 What part of the body is in photograph C? What can you see in D?

2 Which adjectives from the box below can you use to talk about

1 tae kwon do?                    3 going for a walk?
2 yoga?                           4 free diving?

> easy   fast   good   hard   quick   slow   strong   tough

3 🔊 5.1 Listen to three adjectives. What sound is underlined in each one?

1 qui<u>ck</u>              2 stro<u>ng</u>              3 tou<u>gh</u>

4 🔊 5.2 Listen to the words from the box. Put them in the correct column of the table below.

> <u>c</u>ountry   evening   father   mos<u>que</u>   <u>ph</u>one
> <u>ph</u>ysics   si<u>ng</u>er   smo<u>ke</u>   spring

| qui<u>ck</u> | stro<u>ng</u> | tou<u>gh</u> |
|---|---|---|
|  |  |  |
|  |  |  |
|  |  |  |

**5** Work with a partner. In turns, practise saying the sentences.

1 Physics is easier than English.
2 Summer is nicer than spring.
3 Phones are better than computers.
4 Yoga is tougher than free diving.

Do you agree with the sentences?

**6** Read the pairs of sentences in the box below. Then answer questions 1 and 2 about the words in bold.

1 What kind of word are they?    2 What do the words mean?
  a adjectives                     a not tough/strong/good
  b verbs                          b more tough/strong/good

| | |
|---|---|
| Running's a tough sport. | Free diving's **tougher** than running. |
| Mark's a strong man. | Lisa's **stronger** than Steph. |
| Yoga's good for you. | Yoga's **better** for you than tae kwon do. |

EXPLANATION

## Comparative adjectives

Use comparative adjectives to compare two or more things.

### Adjectives with one or two syllables

Add -er (than) to one-syllable adjectives. Use -ier (than) with adjectives with a -y.

Women are **tougher** than men. Free diving is **harder** than running.
Zumba is **healthier** than walking. Yoga is **easier** for women.

Some adjectives double the consonant: *big, fat, fit, thin.*

Men are **bigger than** women. My brother is **fatter than** my sister.

### Adjectives with two or more syllables

Do not add -er. Say *more* ADJECTIVE (*than*).

Football is more **popular** than tennis in my country.
Baseball is more **important** than basketball in my country.

**Note:** Learn these comparative adjectives:
*good* → *better* (than), *bad* → *worse* (than)

# PRONUNCIATION FOR LISTENING

**7** 🔊 5.3 Listen to the pairs of sentences in Exercise 6. Underline the words with stress. Then listen again and repeat.

## WHILE LISTENING

**8** 🔊 **5.4** Listen to a lecture about sport. What is the main topic of the lecture? Circle the correct answer.

   **a** tae kwon do and yoga

   **b** men, women and sport

   **c** the bones in your back

UNLOCK
ONLINE

**9** 🔊 **5.4** Listen again and answer the questions.

   1 What's Dr Hunter's subject?

   2 What's her first question?

   3 Why do her students think men are better in all sports?

   4 Why are women better at yoga?

   5 Which is Dr Hunter's favourite sport?

   6 Why does she think women are better at her favourite sport?

**10** Match the answers (a–f) with the correct questions from Exercise 9 (1–6).

   **a** They learn quicker and they are faster.

   **b** tae kwon do

   **c** They have stronger backs.

   **d** They think men are bigger, stronger, tougher and faster than women.

   **e** Are men better than women in all sports?

   **f** sports science

## PRACTICE

**11** Work with a partner. Take turns to ask and answer the questions in Exercise 9.

# ◎ LANGUAGE DEVELOPMENT

UNLOCK
ONLINE

## VOCABULARY FOR SPORT

Use the words from the box for Exercises 1, 2 and 3.

> base   basket   foot   judo   karate   kung fu
> pilates   running   skiing   swimming   ~~tae kwon do~~
> tennis   volley   yoga   zumba

**1** Write four words in the gaps to make words for sports.

   _____ball       _____ball

   _____ball       _____ball

**2** Put the letters in order to make words for martial arts.

1 AOTDENKOW     _tae kwon do_
2 RAAKET     _____
3 ODJU     _____
4 FUKUGN     _____

**3** Work with a partner. Check the meaning of the words in bold. Then ask and answer the questions. (Choose your answers from the words in the box at the bottom of page 92.)

1 Which sports do you **play in a team**?
2 Which sports can you **do alone**?
3 Which two martial arts are **Japanese**?
4 Which sports usually have two **players**?
5 Can people **score a goal** or **a point** in swimming?
6 Which sports have a **winner** and a **loser**?
7 Which kinds of sport or exercise are **more popular with** women?

## COMPARATIVE ADJECTIVES

**4** Circle the correct words or phrases.

1 Basketball players are _tall / taller_ people.
2 Zumba is _faster than / more fast_ yoga.
3 I think women can run _fast that / faster than_ men.
4 Manchester's football stadium is _biger than / bigger than_ this one.
5 I think Madrid has _a better / a more good_ football team than Manchester.

**5** Correct the mistakes in these sentences.

1 Is football more healthier than yoga?
2 Are men tough women?
3 Are martial arts more easy for men?
4 Is swimming more than dangerous judo?
5 Is tennis popular that basketball in your country?
6 Is running more good than volleyball?

**6** Work with a partner. Ask and answer the questions in Exercise 5.

## PREPARING TO LISTEN

### Using your knowledge

Before you listen to a lecture, answer these questions.

• What is the topic of the lecture?

• What do you know about the topic?

Use your knowledge of the topic to help you understand.

**USING YOUR
KNOWLEDGE**

**1** You are going to listen to a student compare two kinds of sport or exercise. Before you listen, work with a partner. Look at the photographs (a–e) and answer the questions. Use the phrase from the box below to help you.

1 What kinds of sports and exercise can you see?
2 What adjectives from this unit can you use to talk about these kinds of sport and exercise?
3 Which sport or exercise is better for ...
   a children?
   b young men? / young women?
   c old men? / old women?

> I think … is better for …
>
> I think yoga is better for children.

**UNLOCK** LISTENING AND SPEAKING SKILLS 1

**2** Write the comparative adjectives in the gaps. Then match the opposites.

1 healthy _healthier_  [ h ]
2 fit _____  [ ]
3 thin _____  [ ]
4 fast _____  [ ]
5 popular _____  [ ]
6 strong _____  [ ]
7 good _____  [ ]
8 happy _____  [ ]

a fat _____
b bad _____
c unpopular _____
d weak _____
e unfit _____
f unhappy _____
g slow _____
h unhealthy _____

## WHILE LISTENING

**3** 🔊 5.5 Listen and answer the questions.

1 Which two photographs (a–e) does she talk about?
2 Are these kinds of sport or exercise more popular with men or women?

**4** 🔊 5.5 Listen again. Write the adjectives you hear in the gaps.

1 Today, many young people have an _____ lifestyle.
2 They can be _____ .
3 How can we make young people _____ ?
4 Pilates is _____ than zumba.
5 It's _____ for older people.
6 It can make you _____ .

**5** Work with a partner. Compare your answers. Then check your spelling with the adjectives in Exercise 2.

## DISCUSSION

**6** Work with a partner. Compare these pairs of sport and exercise.

1 zumba and pilates
2 pilates and kung fu
3 kung fu and tennis
4 tennis and skiing

# CRITICAL THINKING

At the end of this unit, you are going to do the speaking task below.

> Compare different kinds of sport and exercise.

REMEMBER

**1** Work with a partner. Ask and answer the questions.

1 What sports can you see in the photographs?
2 Do you do any of these sports? Do you watch any of these sports?

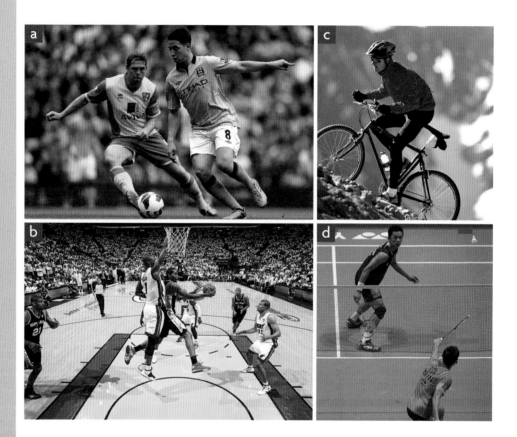

## Use a table to make notes

Use a table to help you organize your knowledge. A table can help you compare two more things or topics. Comparisons can help you

- understand a topic.

- find ideas for a talk on a topic.

**2** Work with a partner. Use the internet to help you find information on the sports in photographs a–d. Make notes in the table.

|  | football | badminton | cycling | basketball |
|---|---|---|---|---|
| one or many people? | many |  |  | many |
| two players or teams? | teams |  |  | teams |
| how many players in a team? | 11 |  | no players |  |
| winners and losers? |  | yes |  |  |
| score goals or points? |  | points | no goals or points |  |
| inside or outside? | outside |  |  | inside |
| places? | a football pitch | a badminton court |  | a basketball court |

**3** Which sports are similar? Which sports are different?

# SPEAKING

## PREPARATION FOR SPEAKING

### PRONUNCIATION FOR SPEAKING

**1** 🔊 **5.6** Listen to and read the statements. What do the parts in bold show?

1 **Bas**-ket-ball is **fas**-ter than **foot**-ball.
2 But is **bas**-ket-ball **bet**-ter than **foot**-ball?
3 A **foot**-ball **team** is **big**-ger than a **bas**-ket-ball team.
4 **Ju**-do is **bet**-ter for **young** men.
5 **Ten**-nis is **bet**-ter for **young** wo men.

**2** 🔊 **5.6** Listen again. Do the parts in red have stress?

**3** 🔊 **5.6** Listen again and repeat.

EXPLANATION

> ### Weak vowel sounds /ə/
> If a syllable does not have stress, it is a weak vowel sound: *faster, better, bigger*

**4** Do you think statements 1–5 in Exercise 1 are true or false?

### MAKING COMPARISONS

**5** Choose the best word for each gap.

1 Football and _____ are similar. They are team games.
  **a** running       **b** swimming       **c** basketball
2 Football and _____ are different.
  **a** cycling       **b** baseball       **c** basketball
3 Cycling is a _____ sport.
  **a** fit          **b** healthy        **c** slow
4 There are no _____ in badminton.
  **a** points       **b** players        **c** goals
5 There are _____ players in basketball than in badminton.
  **a** no           **b** more           **c** five
6 People _____ cycling outside.
  **a** play         **b** go             **c** do

**6** Work with a partner. Match the best pairs.

1 You can play ...           **a** are different.
2 There are no ...           **b** players in volleyball than in tennis.
3 Tennis and skiing ...      **c** teams in skiing.
4 Skiing is a ...            **d** healthy sport.
5 There are more ...         **e** volleyball inside or outside.

**7** Compare football, tennis and running. Use your knowledge and the phrases in Exercises 1–6 to help you.

*Football and tennis are different.*
*There are no goals in running.*

## SPORTS COLLOCATIONS

**8** Write the words from the box in the table.

baseball   horse-riding   judo   rugby   running   yoga

|  | | | | | |
|---|---|---|---|---|---|
| **play** | tennis <br> (1)_____ <br> football <br> basketball <br> (2)_____ | **go** | cycling <br> (3)_____ <br> skiing <br> swimming <br> (4)_____ | **do** | (5)_____ <br> zumba <br> karate <br> kung fu <br> (6)_____ |

## INTRODUCING A TALK

**9** 🔊 **5.7** Read and listen to a student introduce her talk. Six words and phrases are missing.

OK, good afternoon, (1)_____ ! (2)_____ , many young people have an unhealthy lifestyle, and this (3)_____ they can be unhappy. This is a real problem. So (4)_____ start with this question: (5)_____ we make young people (6)_____? How can we make them healthier? Happier?

**10** 🔊 **5.7** Match the words and phrases to the correct gaps. Then listen again and check.

a fitter
b I want to
c everybody
d How can
e means
f Today

**11** 🔊 **5.8** Read and listen to another introduction. Circle the word you hear.

OK, good (1)morning / afternoon everybody!

Today, I want to talk to you about three kinds of (2)sport / exercise.

I want to (3)start / finish with this question.

Which sport is better for (4)old / young men? Which is better for women?

**12** 🔊 **5.8** Listen again. Underline the stress. Then listen and repeat.

## SPEAKING TASK

You are going give a short talk. You will compare different kinds of sport or exercise to answer this question.

> Which kind of sport or exercise is better for young men / young women?

1 Choose three kinds of sport or exercise. Use the internet to find a photograph of each one.

2 Make notes on your choices in the table.

| | 1 _____ | 2 _____ | 3 _____ |
|---|---|---|---|
| one or many people? | | | |
| two players or teams? | | | |
| how many players in a team? | | | |
| winners and losers? | | | |
| score goals or points? | | | |
| inside or outside? | | | |
| places? | | | |

3 Choose adjectives to talk about your choices. Then write the comparative adjectives for each one.

| | 1 _____ | 2 _____ | 3 _____ |
|---|---|---|---|
| adjective<br>*fast* | | | |
| comparative<br>*faster (than)* | | | |

**UNL OCK** LISTENING AND SPEAKING SKILLS 1

**4** Use the adjectives to compare your choices. Write sentences or make notes.

**5** Practise your talk. Record yourself if you can.

• Introduce your talk (see Exercise 9 on page 99).
• Compare the different kinds of sport or exercise.
• Answer this question: *Which kind of sport or exercise is better for young men / young women?*

**6** Work in groups.

1 Take turns to give your talk to your group.
2 When it is your turn to listen, make notes in this table.

PRACTISE

PRESENT

| student | Aysa | | | |
|---|---|---|---|---|
| description of sport or exercise and rules | • karate, 2 people indoors<br>• running, 1 or 20 people race, fast, outdoors, no points | | | |
| better for young men? | karate | | | |
| better for young women? | running | | | |

| TASK CHECKLIST | ✔ |
| --- | --- |
| Did you compare different kinds of sport and exercise? | |
| Did you make comparisons? | |
| Did you use comparative adjectives (e.g. *faster – slower*, *stronger – weaker*)? | |
| Did you pronounce *-er* and *than* with a weak vowel (/ə/)? | |

## OBJECTIVES REVIEW

*I can ...*

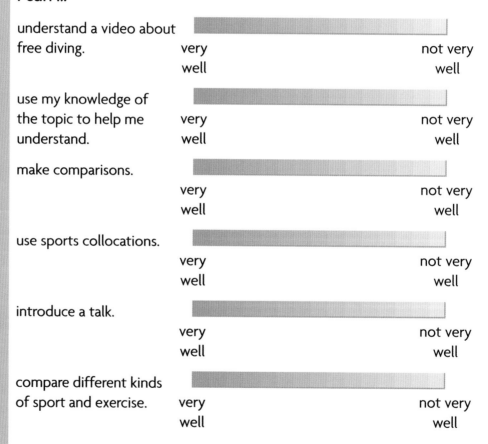

understand a video about free diving.

very well        not very well

use my knowledge of the topic to help me understand.

very well        not very well

make comparisons.

very well        not very well

use sports collocations.

very well        not very well

introduce a talk.

very well        not very well

compare different kinds of sport and exercise.

very well        not very well

# WORDLIST

| UNIT VOCABULARY | |
|---|---|
| alone (adj) | player (n) |
| ancient (adj) | point (n) |
| back (n) | popular (adj) |
| badminton (n) | professional (adj) |
| badminton court (n) | quick (adj) |
| baseball (n) | rugby (n) |
| basketball (n) | running (n) |
| basketball court (n) | score (n) |
| bone (n) | skiing (n) |
| competition (n) | slow (adj) |
| cycling (n) | strong (adj) |
| fan (n) | swimming (n) |
| fast (adj) | tae kwon do (n) |
| fat (adj) | tall (adj) |
| fit (adj) | team (n) |
| football (n) | tennis (n) |
| football pitch (n) | thin (adj) |
| goal (n) | tough (adj) |
| good (adj) | traditional (adj) |
| hard (adj) | unfit (adj) |
| horse-riding (n) | unhappy (adj) |
| Japanese (adj) | unhealthy (adj) |
| judo (n) | volleyball (n) |
| karate (n) | weak (adj) |
| kung fu (n) | winner (n) |
| loser (n) | yoga (n) |
| million (n) | zumba (n) |
| pilates (n) | |

## LEARNING OBJECTIVES

| | |
|---|---|
| Watch and listen | Watch and understand a video about fire rangers |
| Listening skills | Listen for opinion |
| Speaking skills | *have/has to* |
| Speaking task | Choose a person for a job |

**UNLOCK YOUR KNOWLEDGE**

1 Which job can you see in the photograph?

2 Which adjectives describe the job in the photograph?

   boring   dangerous   difficult   easy   interesting   safe

3 Would you like to do this job? Why? / Why not?

# WATCH AND LISTEN

    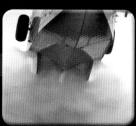

## PREPARING TO WATCH

UNDERSTANDING KEY VOCABULARY

**1** You are going to watch a video about fire rangers. Before you watch, match the words in bold in the sentences (1–4) with the definitions below (a–d).

1 The water **puts out** the fire. _____
2 The plane **picks up** water. _____
3 The plane **takes off**. _____
4 Water **drops** out of the plane. _____

a The plane goes up into the air.
b The plane collects water.
c Water goes out of the plane down to the ground.
d The water stops the fire burning.

**2** Look at the four images from the video and describe them using verbs from Exercise 1.

**3** Write the verbs from the box in the gaps.

> drop    pick up    put out    take off

1 Don't use water to _____ a fire in your kitchen. It can be very dangerous.
2 Please don't _____ that vase. I don't want it to break.
3 Your plane is going to _____ at 5 am and arrive in Brazil at 2.30 pm.
4 Can you _____ your books, please? We're going to change classrooms.

**4** How can we measure these things? Match the pairs.

1 speed          a litres
2 weight        b kilos
3 time            c kilometres per hour
4 water          d minutes

UNL**O**CK LISTENING AND SPEAKING SKILLS 1

# WHILE WATCHING

**5** ▶ Watch the video. Then write the phrases from the box in the correct column of the table below.

> picks up water    sends information    takes a call about the fire
> takes off first    takes off second

| The CL2–15 plane crew | The helicopter crew | The fire centre |
|---|---|---|
| 1 _____ | 3 _____ | 5 _____ |
| 2 _____ | 4 _____ | |

**6** ▶ Watch again. Write the correct number in the gaps to answer these questions.

1 How fast does the plane fly over the lake?
_____ kilometres per hour

2 How many litres of water does the plane pick up?
_____ litres

3 How long does it take for the plane to pick up more water?
_____ minutes

4 How many times does the plane have to pick up water?
_____ times

**7** Work with a partner. Take turns to ask and answer the questions in Exercise 6.

**8** Read the questions and circle the correct answers.

1 CL2–15 pilots have to be very experienced because they have to
  a work very fast.
  b fly old planes.
  c do a dangerous job.
2 What is the most dangerous time for the CL2–15 crew?
  a when they pick up water
  b when they fly close to the forest
  c when they drop water

# DISCUSSION

**9** Work with a partner. Discuss the questions.

1 Would you like to be a fire ranger? Why? / Why not?
2 What job would you like to do?

## LISTENING 1

### PREPARING TO LISTEN

UNDERSTANDING
KEY VOCABULARY

**1** You are going to listen to a student ask for help. Before you listen, match the jobs (a–f) in the box to the correct picture (1–6).

a lawyer ☐　　c engineer ☐　　e musician ☐
b banker ☐　　d pilot ☐　　f scientist ☐

**2** 🔊 6.1 Listen to the jobs. Write the number of syllables, then mark the stress.

**3** Answer the questions about the jobs in Exercise 1. Use your own ideas.

Who
1 works harder than other people? *a lawyer, ...*
2 helps people?
3 has a more interesting job?
4 earns more money?

---

**EXPLANATION**

### Listening for opinion

An opinion is an idea about a person, place, thing or event. We can use *should* to give advice and *think* to give an opinion.

What should I do? Should I study Turkish?
You should work hard.
I think you should watch videos in English.
I don't think you should drink a lot of coffee.

**4** Look at the conversations and write *should* or *think* in the gaps.

   **a** **A:** Can I help you?
       **B:** Yes. I want to speak good English. What (1)_____ I do?
       **A:** I (2)_____ you (3)_____ learn five new words every day.
       **B:** Good idea!

   **b** **A:** Hello, Philip. How can I help you?
       **B:** Well, I want to study a foreign language. But I don't know what to
           do. (4)_____ I study Turkish? Or German? Or Chinese?
       **A:** Well, I don't (5)_____ you (6)_____ study German or
           Chinese. Your father has a business in Istanbul. So I (7)_____
           you (8)_____ study Turkish.
       **B:** That's great, thanks!

**5** 🔊 6.2 Listen and check.

## PRONUNCIATION FOR LISTENING

**6** 🔊 6.3 Listen and repeat the phrases in the Explanation box on page 108.

## WHILE LISTENING

**7** 🔊 6.4 You are going to listen to a student ask for advice. Circle the jobs you hear from Exercise 1.

> **LISTENING FOR MAIN IDEAS**
>
>

**8** Now circle the correct answers.

   **1** Who is the student with?
     **a** her friend
     **b** her teacher
     **c** her mother

   **2** What does the student ask for?
     **a** money
     **b** to be a musician
     **c** advice about what to study

**9** 🔊 6.4 Listen again. Circle the correct answers.

> **LISTENING FOR DETAIL**

   **1** The student is going to college *next year / this year*.
   **2** There are many jobs for *teachers / musicians*.
   **3** The student says a doctor's life is *good / boring*.
   **4** The student's mother wants her to go to *law school / medical school*.
   **5** The teacher says the student has *good grades / a good job*.
   **6** The teacher thinks the student should *go to law school / get a job*.

## DISCUSSION

**10** Work with a partner. What should the student do?

> I think she should + VERB
>
> I don't think she should + VERB

## VOCABULARY FOR JOBS

EXPLANATION

### Suffixes

We can use a suffix to make new words for jobs.

music + –ian = musician
police + –man = policeman
build + –er = builder

**1** Work with a partner. Think of more jobs for each suffix.

**2** Compare your answers with the class.

**3** Work with a partner. Ask and answer the questions.

1 Would you like to do any of the jobs you thought of in Exercise 1? Why? / Why not?
2 What is your dream job?
3 What do you have to do to get this job?

UNLOCK ONLINE

## ADJECTIVES FOR PEOPLE

**4** Write the adjectives from the box in the correct column of the table below.

clever   good-looking   fit   friendly   helpful
interesting   kind   polite   strong   slim

| body | character |
|------|-----------|
| good-looking | clever |
| | |

**5** Circle the best adjectives.

    1 A good policeman should be *good-looking* / *fit.*

    2 A good lawyer should be *clever* / *friendly.*

    3 A good doctor should be *slim* / *kind.*

    4 A good nurse should be *interesting* / *helpful.*

    5 A good waiter should be *polite* / *strong.*

**6** Work with a partner. Think of some more adjectives to add to Exercise 4.

**7** Work with a partner. Use the adjectives to talk about the jobs you thought of in Exercise 1.

*A good teacher should be interesting.*

*A good fireman should be strong.*

## COLLOCATIONS FOR JOBS

**8** Complete the descriptions with the correct jobs.

> architect  builder  engineer  farmer
> lawyer  pilot  scientist  waiter

    1 A _____ builds houses.

    2 A _____ does experiments.

    3 A _____ practises law.

    4 An _____ designs roads and bridges.

    5 A _____ flies a plane.

    6 An _____ designs houses and buildings.

    7 A _____ works on a farm.

    8 A _____ serves food and drink in a café or restaurant.

  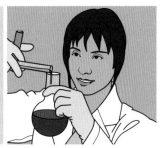

## PREPARING TO LISTEN

**PREDICTING
CONTENT**

**1** You are going to listen to two managers choose somebody for a job. Before you listen, read the jobs website below and answer the questions.

1 Where is the job?
2 What is the job?
3 What does *has experience* mean?
4 What kind of person should apply?

**Home** > **Jobs** > **Current vacancies**

**Fitness instructor
(Ref: UoY-SSv/SpC-0098)**

The UoY sports centre is looking for a new fitness instructor. We are looking for a person who:

• can teach sport and exercise.
• is friendly and helpful.
• has experience.

**About you**
You should:

• be fit and strong.
• know three or more sports.
• speak English and French.

Click here to apply.

**About us**
The UoY sports centre is for students and staff at UoY. We have sports for men and women here. We have a gym, a swimming pool, tennis courts, a football pitch, and a basketball court.

We have courses in yoga, pilates, zumba, kung-fu, running, cycling, swimming, and many more.

**UNL⌀CK** LISTENING AND SPEAKING SKILLS 1

**2** Work with a partner. Read about a person who wants the job. Then ask and answer the questions below.

Student A: Turn to page 195.
Student B: Turn to page 197.

1 Is it a man or a woman?
2 What's his/her name?
3 Where's he/she from?
4 What languages does he/she speak?
5 What sports can he/she teach?

**3** Read your partner's text (Alan Green or Lucy Lau). Who should get the job?

## WHILE LISTENING

**4** ◀) 6.5 Listen to two managers choose a new fitness instructor. Who do they choose, Alan or Lucy?

**5** ◀) 6.5 Read questions 1–6. Then listen again and circle the correct answers.

LISTENING FOR
DETAIL

1 What other job do they talk about?
  **a** nurse     **b** scientist     **c** accountant
2 Paul thinks a good fitness instructor should
  **a** be fit and strong.
  **b** be a good teacher.
  **c** teach tennis.
3 Paul likes Lucy because she's
  **a** a good scientist.
  **b** Canadian.
  **c** a fitness instructor.
4 Emma thinks a fitness instructor has to be
  **a** friendly and helpful.
  **b** fit and strong.
  **c** kind and polite.
5 Emma thinks Alan can help students
  **a** work hard.
  **b** be polite.
  **c** have good ideas.
6 Paul thinks Lucy is better because she
  **a** has experience.
  **b** can teach popular sports.
  **c** can speak Cantonese.

## DISCUSSION

**6** Do you agree with Paul? Why? / Why not?

# CRITICAL THINKING

At the end of this unit, you are going to do the speaking task below.

> Choose a person for a job.

EXPLANATION

## Choose criteria

Criteria are reasons for choosing something. Here are two examples from Listening 2:

> I want a person who has experience, a person who can teach me tennis or volleyball.
> We want a person who can make the students work hard.

APPLY

1 Read about another job and answer the questions.

1 What is the job?
2 What are the job criteria?
3 What kind of person do they want?

Home > Jobs > **Current vacancies**

**Sports Centre Nurse
(Ref: UoY-SSv/SpC-0099)**

The UoY sports centre is looking for a new nurse. We are looking for a person who:

- has experience
- _____
- _____
- _____

**About you**

You should be:

- helpful
- _____
- _____
- _____

Click here to apply.

**Home**

**Jobs**

Register for job adverts

Manage job alerts

FAQ

Contact us

**2** Work in groups. Answer the questions.

1 What does a nurse have to do?
2 What kind of person should a good nurse be?

**3** Choose three more criteria from each column. Add them to the website.

| We are looking for a person who: | You should be: |
|---|---|
| • ~~has experience~~ | • clever |
| • works in a big hospital | • fit |
| • loves sport | • friendly |
| • does yoga | • polite |
| • helps doctors | • kind |
| • has a degree | • ~~helpful~~ |
| • likes children | • strong |

# SPEAKING

## PREPARATION FOR SPEAKING

### HAVE/HAS TO

**1** 🔊 6.6 Listen and write the words you hear in the gaps. Use the words from the box to help you.

> have    has    have to    has to

1 Fatima _____ two jobs.
2 Mehmet _____ work very hard.
3 I _____ a very good job.
4 Engineers _____ a difficult job.
5 Paul _____ an important job.
6 Builders _____ work fast.
7 Emma _____ choose a new fitness instructor.
8 Lawyers _____ be clever.

**2** Look at the sentences in Exercise 1 again. What kind of word or phrase is after

1 *have* and *has*?
2 *have to* and *has to*?

## *have to*

Use *have to / has to* + VERB and to show that something is necessary.

*Nurses have to be helpful.*
*A farmer has to get up early.*
*Do waiters have to be polite?*

Use *don't/doesn't have to* + VERB to show that something is not necessary.

*Nurses don't have to be women.*
*An architect doesn't have to build houses.*

**3** Correct the mistakes in the statements.

1 Students have read a lot of books.
2 My teacher have to walk to school.
3 You don't have study English.
4 Teachers don't to work at night.
5 Have we learn this grammar?
6 What does a nurse has to do?

## PRONUNCIATION FOR SPEAKING

**4** ◀)6.6 Listen to the sentences in Exercise 1 again. How do we pronounce the letters in bold below?

1 *have to*
2 *has to*
3 *have*
4 *has*

**5** Match the correct sound (a–d) to the verbs in Exercise 4 (1–4).

a /f/      b /v/      c /z/      d /s/

**6** Work with a partner. Choose one of these people each. What do they have to do?

journalist   pilot   policeman   scientist

**7** Work with a new partner. Repeat Exercise 6, choosing a different job.

# SPEAKING TASK

You are going to choose a person to be a nurse in the University of Yukon Sports Centre (see Critical thinking, page 114).

1  Work in groups of three.

Student A: Read about Inesh (below).
Student B: Read about Morena (page 118).
Student C: Read about Darren (page 118).

PREPARE

## Student A

Home > Jobs > **Current vacancies**

**About you**

My name's Inesh and I'm from Yogyakarta, Indonesia. I speak four languages: Indonesian, Chinese, Spanish and English. I speak Spanish better than English.

I'm studying to be a nurse in a big hospital in Jakarta.

I'm polite and friendly. This is important, because nurses have to help doctors and work with patients.

I would like to go to Canada and work in your Sports Centre after my degree.

## Student B

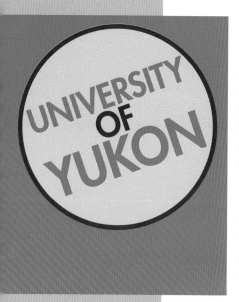

Home > Jobs > **Current vacancies**

**About you**

My name's Morena and I'm from São Paulo in Brazil. I speak Portuguese, Spanish and English.

I'm a nurse in a children's hospital. I like working with children, but I would like to work in your Sports Centre in Canada.

I'm a friendly and helpful nurse. I love sports. I go running and do yoga. I'm fit and strong. This is important because nurses have to work hard.

## Student C

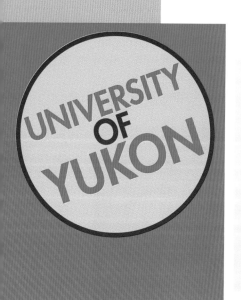

Home > Jobs > **Current vacancies**

**About you**

My name's Darren and I'm from Manchester in England. I'm a nurse in a big hospital. I work hard and I'm good at my job.

I don't speak French, but I'm clever and a good student.

I'm fit and healthy. I love football and basketball and I go to a gym. This is important, because a sports-centre nurse should do sports.

I would like to live in Canada.

**UNLƏCK** LISTENING AND SPEAKING SKILLS 1

**2** Ask and answer the questions. Use the phrases on the right to help you.

1  Where's he/she from?        He's/She's from ... in ...

He/She speaks ...

2  What languages does he/she speak?        He/She can't speak ...

3  Is he/she a student? (Where is he/she a student?)        Yes, he/she's a student in ...        No, he/she isn't.

4  Does he/she work in a hospital? (Where does he/she work?)        Yes, he/she works in ...        No, he/she doesn't.

5  What does he/she think is important?        He/She thinks it's important to ... because a nurse ...

**3** Work in your group of three. Who should be the new nurse?

- Ask for opinions: What do you think?
- Give opinions: I think ... should be the new nurse.
- Give reasons: ... because he/she ...

**4** Tell the class your answers.

We think that ... should be the new nurse because he/she ...

## TASK CHECKLIST                                                    ✔

| Did you choose a person for a job? | |
| --- | --- |
| Did you give reasons for your opinions? | |
| Did you use *think*, *should* and *have to*? | |
| Did you use /v/ and /s/ to pronounce *have to* and *has to*? | |

## OBJECTIVES REVIEW

*I can ...*

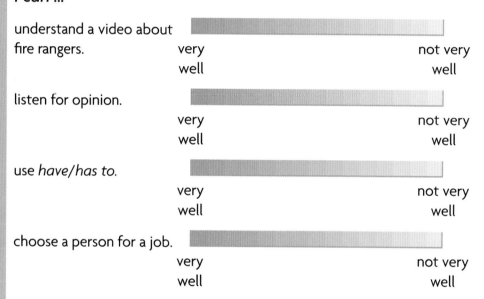

understand a video about
fire rangers.

very well                                                      not very well

listen for opinion.

very well                                                      not very well

use *have/has to*.

very well                                                      not very well

choose a person for a job.

very well                                                      not very well

# WORDLIST

| UNIT VOCABULARY | |
| --- | --- |
| accountant (n) | helpful (adj) |
| architect (n) | kind (adj) |
| banker (n) | lawyer (n) |
| boring (adj) | musician (n) |
| builder (n) | nurse (n) |
| clever (adj) | opinion (n) |
| engineer (n) | pilot (n) |
| experience (n) | policeman (n) |
| farmer (n) | reason (n) |
| fire (n) | slim (adj) |
| fireman (n) | take off (v) |
| friendly (adv) | time (n) |
| good-looking (adj) | waiter (n) |

## LEARNING OBJECTIVES

| Watch and listen | Watch and understand a video about a place in Mumbai, India |
|---|---|
| Listening skills | Listen for reasons |
| Speaking skills | Ask for and give an opinion; agree and disagree |
| Speaking task | Discuss ideas for a new building |

## UNLOCK YOUR KNOWLEDGE

1 Choose three words from the box to describe the photograph.

African   Asian   European   faraway   interesting
normal   traditional   unusual

2 How is the house in the photograph the same as other houses?
It has a roof.

# WATCH AND LISTEN

## PREPARING TO WATCH

UNDERSTANDING KEY VOCABULARY

**1** You are going to watch a video about a place in Mumbai, India. Before you watch, read the phrases below. Then write the words in bold next to the correct definitions.

1 _____ : a large group of people who come together (n)
2 _____ : a place where people make bread, cakes, baklava, etc. (n)
3 _____ : putting colour on something, e.g. a house, a wall, a door (v)
4 _____ : a poor part of a city where a lot of people live (n)
5 _____ : when there is a small space between two sides (adj)
6 _____ : when there are a lot of people in a place (adj)

**a** ☐ men working in a **bakery**

**b** ☐ an important man with a **crowd** of people

**c** ☐ a **crowded** train station

**d** ☐ men **painting** walls

**e** ☐ children running in **narrow** streets

**f** ☐ a big city at night

**g** ☐ people living in a **slum**

**2** ▶ Watch the video without sound. Put the images from the video (a–g) in the order you see them.

**3** Work with a partner. What do you think the video is about? Circle the best answer.

I think the main topic of the video is
a information about how to build a slum house.
b information about life in a slum.
c information about schools in a slum.
d the story of one important man in the slum.
e the story of one family in the slum.

## WHILE WATCHING

**4** ▶ Watch again with sound. Check your answer to Exercise 3.

**5** ▶ Watch again. Are the statements true (T) or false (F)?

UNDERSTANDING
MAIN IDEAS

UNDERSTANDING
DETAIL

1 A lot of people live in slums in Mumbai. _____
2 There are only houses in the Dharavi slum. _____
3 Businesses make a lot of money in the Dharavi slum. _____
4 Krishna is a TV presenter. _____
5 Sushila and her family need a new home. _____
6 Sushila pays Krishna to build a new home for her family. _____
7 Sushila has no children. _____
8 Sushila's family don't like their new home. _____

## DISCUSSION

**6** Read the text in the box. What do you think? Should the people leave the Dharavi slum?

The government wants people to leave the Dharavi slum and live in modern apartments. Krishna and other people do not want to leave the slum.

# LISTENING 1

## PREPARING TO LISTEN

UNDERSTANDING
KEY VOCABULARY

**1** You are going to listen to an interview on the radio. Before you listen, match the pairs.

| | |
|---|---|
| 1 A psychologist | a manages a restaurant. |
| 2 An architect | b studies how people think. |
| 3 A restaurant manager | c designs buildings. |

**2** Check the meaning of the words in bold in 1–8 below. Then choose answers from the box.

> Yes, it does.  Yes, they do.  Yes, it is.  Yes, they are.
> Yes, it can.  No, it can't.  dirty  sad

1 What is the opposite of *clean*?
2 What is the opposite of *happy*?
3 Does exercise make you feel **thirsty**?
4 Do photographs of food make you feel **hungry**?
5 Is *a flat* the **same** as *an apartment*?
6 Is **fresh** food **healthy**?
7 Are Dubai and Warsaw in **different** countries?
8 Can good food **change the way** you feel?

**3** Work with a partner. Take turns to ask and answer the questions in Exercise 2.

## PRONUNCIATION FOR LISTENING

**4** 🔊 **71** Read the phrases (1–6) from the interview. How do we pronounce the red and blue letters? Listen, then circle the correct answer (a–c) below.

1 an author of many books
2 I help architects.
3 For example
4 good ideas
5 restaurants in London
6 What about England?

a We do not pronounce the red letters.
b We do not pronounce the blue letters.
c We pronounce the red and blue letters together.

EXPLANATION

### Linking words

Link consonant sounds to vowel sounds.

Krishna lives_in_India.
Because_it's_a good_idea.

# WHILE LISTENING

**5** 🔊 **7.2** Listen to an interivew on the radio. Circle the correct answers.

LISTENING FOR
MAIN IDEAS

UNL♂CK
ONLINE

1  Dr Thompson is
   **a** a psychologist.   **b** an architect.   **c** a restaurant manager.
2  Many Mexican restaurants have
   **a** orange walls.   **b** red walls.   **c** white walls.
3  Many Chinese restaurants have
   **a** orange walls.   **b** red walls.   **c** white walls.
4  The main topic of the interview is
   **a** buildings.   **b** colours.   **c** restaurants.

## Listening for reasons

Reasons are facts or opinions about why something happens. Reasons are important information. Listen carefully when you hear the words *why* and *because*.

**6** Match the reasons (a–e) to the correct questions (1–5).

LISTENING FOR
DETAIL

1  Why is colour important?
2  Why do many restaurants in Mexico have orange walls?
3  Why don't many restaurants in London have orange walls?
4  Why do many Chinese restaurants have red walls?
5  Why is white a good colour for an English restaurant?

a  Because this is the colour of fire and good things.
b  Because it changes the way people think and feel.
c  Because colours mean different things in different countries.
d  Because this colour makes people feel hungry.
e  Because this colour means fresh and clean.

**7** 🔊 **7.2** Listen again and check your answers.

# DISCUSSION

**8** Work with a partner. Ask and answer the questions.

1  Do you have a favourite colour?
2  What colour is your house?
3  What colour is your room at home?
4  Would you like to change the colour of your house/room?
   What colour would you like to have?

# ⊙ LANGUAGE DEVELOPMENT

UNLOCK ONLINE

## VOCABULARY FOR ROOMS

**1** Work with a partner. Take turns to ask and answer the questions. Use the phrases from the box below to help you.

What's the name of the place where
1  you sleep?
2  you study with other students?
3  you discuss ideas in a group?
4  the family meets (the main room in a house)?
5  you hear lectures?
6  you can use computers?
7  you can study a language on your own?
8  you wash?

> It's a ...    I don't know that one.

**2** Use the words from the box to make new words for rooms.

> centre    hall    lab    room

a  lecture _____
b  class _____
c  language _____
d  bed _____
e  living _____
f  computer _____
g  bath _____
h  seminar _____

**3** Match the words for rooms in Exercise 2 to the correct definitions in Exercise 1.

**4** Work with a partner. Repeat Exercise 1. Are any of your answers different this time?

**5** Write the words from Exercise 2 in two groups.

1  places in a house:

_____

2  places in a university:

_____

## ADJECTIVES FOR FURNITURE

**6** Work with a partner. Look only at the photographs. Then take turns to ask and answer the question.

> What's this in English?    It's a ... / I'm not sure.

a comfortable _____

a glass _____

a leather _____

a plastic _____

a wooden _____

a brown _____

a soft _____

a metal _____

**7** Write the words from the box in the gaps in Exercise 6.

> armchair   bed   bookcase   chair
> coffee table   study desk   lamp   sofa

**8** Look at the phrases in Exercise 6. Find four more different words for materials.

*glass, ...*

## PREPARING TO LISTEN

**UNDERSTANDING KEY VOCABULARY**

**1** You are going to listen to two men discuss ideas for a new building. Before you listen, write the words from the box in the gaps below. Use the words in bold to help you.

> cheap    comfortable    far    quiet

1 I don't think we should go to an **expensive** hotel. I think we should go to a _____ one.
2 That restaurant is very **noisy**. It's not going to be _____ if we go there.
3 My chair isn't very **good**. I'm going to get a more _____ one.
4 'Is your office **near** the train station?'
  'No, it's quite _____ from there.'

**2** Read the sentences in the box below. Then answer the questions.

1 Are the words in blue nouns, verbs or adjectives?
2 Which phrase in yellow means
  **a** a lot?              **b** a little?              **c** not a lot?

> This building is quite modern.    This café is not very cheap.
> This chair is very comfortable.

## WHILE LISTENING

**LISTENING FOR MAIN IDEAS**

UNLOCK ONLINE

**3** 🔊 **7.3** Look at the map of a town on the next page. Then listen to two men discuss ideas for a new building and circle the correct answers.

1 What kind of building do they discuss?
  **a** a train station
  **b** a new office
  **c** a new hotel
2 Where is the new building going to be?
  **a** near the train station
  **b** in the town centre
  **c** near the park
3 Which of these statements is true?
  **a** They agree with every idea.
  **b** They agree with some ideas.
  **c** They don't agree with any ideas.

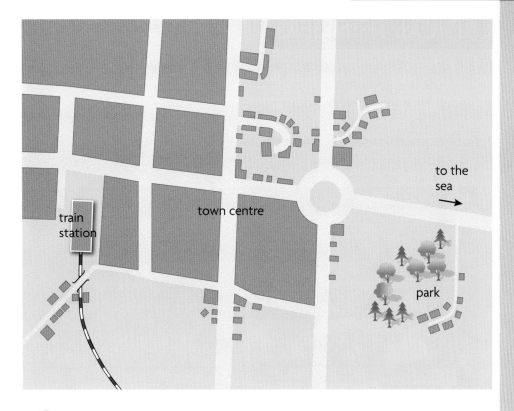

**4** 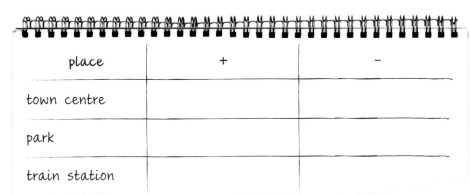 Listen again. Make notes in the table about the points for (+) and against (–) each place. Then answer the questions below.

| place | + | – |
|---|---|---|
| town centre | | |
| park | | |
| train station | | |

1 Are the windows going to be big or small?
2 Are the walls going to be blue or yellow?

**5** Work in groups. Compare your notes. Do you have the same answers?

## DISCUSSION

**6** Work with a partner. Do you agree with the two men? Why? / Why not?

# CRITICAL THINKING

At the end of this unit, you are going to do the speaking task below.

Discuss ideas for a new building.

UNDERSTAND

**1** Look at photographs of three restaurants. Which restaurant is

1 under the sea?　　　2 in the sky?　　　3 in the sea?

At.mosphere, Dubai

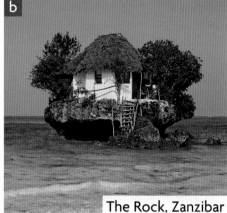

The Rock, Zanzibar

Ithaa, the Maldives

**2** Which restaurant would like to go to? Why? Which restaurant would you not like to go to? Why?

## Find reasons for and against

Before you discuss something, find reasons for (positive) and against (negative).
Record your ideas in a list or table to use during your discussion.

**3** You are going to open a new restaurant. Find reasons for and against each type of restaurant (a, b or c). Then add them to the table below. Use the phrases in the box to help you.

> It's expensive to eat there.     It's far away.
> It's easy to go there.     There are not many tables.
> It's popular with tourists.     It's expensive to build.
> You can't go there when the weather is bad.
> People can take beautiful photographs.
> It's an interesting building.

| place | + | – |
|-------|---|---|
| a |   |   |
| b |   |   |
| c |   |   |

**4** Work with a partner. Which kind of restaurant (a, b or c) would you like to open?

# SPEAKING

 UNLOCK ONLINE

## PREPARATION FOR SPEAKING

1 🔊 7.4 Listen to and read three parts of Listening 2.

**1**

Dale: OK, so we need a place for our new office. <u>What about here?</u>
Hakan: Where?
Dale: The town centre. <u>What do you think?</u>
Hakan: Well, <u>it's a good place. It's near some good roads.</u> But … <u>I don't think we should go there.</u>
Dale: Oh? <u>Why not?</u>
Hakan: <u>Because the buildings in the town centre are very old. They are cold in winter and hot in summer. They're not comfortable places.</u>

**2**

Dale: <u>What about here?</u>
Hakan: The park?
Dale: Yes. <u>It's quiet and it's not far from a big road. What do you think?</u>
Hakan: Hmm, <u>I'm not sure. It's quite far from the town.</u> <u>What about here?</u> Near the train station?
Dale: <u>The train station is good. It's good for travel</u> … but <u>I think we should go to the park. The buildings near the train station aren't cheap.</u>

**3**

Hakan: Now <u>what about the design? I think we should have big windows.</u> <u>What about you?</u>
Dale: <u>Yes, I agree. Big windows are good.</u>

2 Write the underlined phrases in the correct column of the table.

| give a reason | give an opinion | agree or disagree | ask for an opinion |
|---|---|---|---|
| | | | |

**UNL○CK** LISTENING AND SPEAKING SKILLS 1

## ASKING FOR AN OPINION

**3** Write the correct word or phrase from the box in the gaps below.

blue    Indian food    think    you

1  I like modern buildings. What about _____ ?
2  We want to paint the classroom. What about _____ ?
3  I'm going to open a new café. What do you _____ ?
4  Do you want to go to a restaurant this evening? What about _____ ?

**4** Stand up. Ask the questions in Exercise 3 to different students in the class.

## GIVING AN OPINION

**5** You are going to open a new school. Write four opinions. Use the phrases in the box below to help you.

I think we should have small classrooms.
1  I think we should _____ .
2  I think we should _____ .
3  I don't think we should _____ .
4  I don't think we should _____ .

have *big / small* classrooms.
go to a *modern / traditional* building.
have an English class every *day / week*.
open the school in *a city / the country*.
have *computers / books* in class.
study in the *mornings / evenings*.

## AGREEING AND DISAGREEING

**6** Do these sentences express agreement (A) or disagreement (D)?

1  I'm not sure.          ☐        3  I don't agree.   ☐
2  Yes, you're right.   ☐        4  I agree.          ☐

**7** Work with a partner. Take turns to be Student A and Student B.

**Student A:** Give an opinion from Exercise 5. Then ask for an opinion.
I think we should have big classrooms. What do you think?
I don't think we should have computers in class. What about you?

**Student B:** Agree or disagree with Student A.
Yes, I agree.
I'm not sure. I think we should have small classrooms.

# SPEAKING TASK

For Exercises 8–11, work with a partner.

PREPARE

**1** Look at the map of Green Town and read the information in the box below. Then answer the questions.

1 What are you going to do?
2 Where is Green Town?
3 What kind of place is Green Town?
4 What does *go on a day trip* mean? Circle the correct answer.
   a travel on a kind of boat
   b visit a place for one day
   c play a kind of game
5 What do A, B, C and D show you?

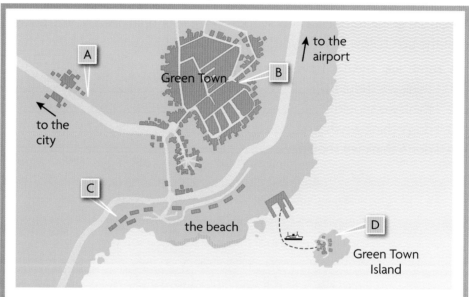

You are going to open a new restaurant in Green Town.

Green Town is a small town near the sea. There are two busy roads near the town. One road goes to the capital city, and the other goes to the airport.

Green Town is very popular with tourists. Tourists come from the capital city and from countries around the world. There are ten big hotels on the beach.

Green Town Island is also popular. Many tourists go on a day trip to the island. Other tourists stay in one of the the island's three small hotels.

Here are four places for your restaurant:

A near the busy main road
B in the town
C on the beach
D on Green Town Island

PRACTISE

**2** Where are you going to put your restaurant? Use the phrases from the box below to help you.

- Choose one place (A–D).
- Give a reason for your answer.

| | |
|---|---|
| What do you think? | It's near the sea. |
| What about ...? | There are a lot of hotels here. |
| I think we should go here. | It's near a busy road. |
| I think ... is the best place. | There are a lot of people in the town. |
| Why? | Many tourists go on a day trip to the island. |
| Because ... | |
| Yes, I agree. | |

**3** What kind of restaurant is it going to be? Use the phrases from the box below to help you.

- Choose a kind of restaurant.
- Give a reason for your answer.

| | |
|---|---|
| What about ... ? | an Arabic restaurant |
| I think it should be a ... | a Chinese restaurant |
| Yes, I agree. | an English restaurant |
| | an Indian restaurant |
| | a Japanese restaurant |

**4** What kind of building is it going to be? Choose a design for the building. Use the phrases from the box to help you.

| | | | | |
|---|---|---|---|---|
| I think we should have | (a) big<br>(a) small | restaurant.<br>windows. | | |
| The walls should be | wooden.<br>metal. | blue.<br>white. | yellow.<br>green. | |
| The tables and chairs should be | plastic.<br>red. | orange. | brown. | |

**5** Now work on your own. Practise your answers to Exercises 2–4.

**6** Work with a new partner. Discuss your ideas for a new restaurant. Choose

- a place.
- the kind of food.
- a name.
- the design.

**7** Tell the class your ideas.

PRESENT

| TASK CHECKLIST | ✔ |
|---|---|
| Did you discuss ideas for a new building? | |
| Did you find reasons for and against? | |
| Did you ask for and give opinions? | |
| Did you agree and disagree? | |
| Did you link consonant sounds with vowel sounds? | |

## OBJECTIVES REVIEW

*I can ...*

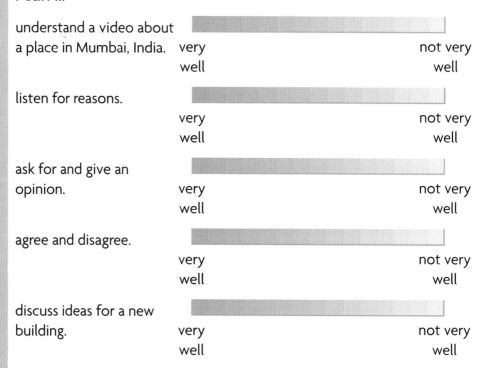

understand a video about
a place in Mumbai, India.

very well — not very well

listen for reasons.

very well — not very well

ask for and give an
opinion.

very well — not very well

agree and disagree.

very well — not very well

discuss ideas for a new
building.

very well — not very well

# WORDLIST

| UNIT VOCABULARY | |
| --- | --- |
| agree (v) | metal (adj) |
| apartment (n) | narrow (adj) |
| change (v) | near (adj) |
| cheap (adj) | noisy (adj) |
| clean (adj) | normal (adj) |
| collect (v) | paint (v) |
| comfortable (adj) | pay (v) |
| day trip (n) | plastic (adj) |
| different (adj) | psychologist (n) |
| dirty (adj) | quiet (adj) |
| disagree (v) | quite (adv) |
| expensive (adj) | roof (n) |
| far (away) (adj) | sad (adj) |
| fresh (adj) | same (adj) |
| glass (adj) | thirsty (adj) |
| hungry (adj) | traditional (adj) |
| leather (adj) | way (n) |
| manage (v) | wooden (adj) |
| manager (v) | |

## LEARNING OBJECTIVES

| Watch and listen | Watch and understand a video about food in China |
|---|---|
| Listening skills | Listen for numbers |
| Speaking skills | Introduce a report; talk about the results |
| Speaking task | Report the results of a survey |

## UNL⌀CK YOUR KNOWLEDGE

Work with a partner. Ask and answer the questions.

1 What can you see in the photograph?
2 Do you often buy things like this?
3 Could the photograph have been taken in your country?

# WATCH AND LISTEN

## PREPARING TO WATCH

**1** You are going to watch a video about food in China. Write the words from the box next to the correct picture.

> beans   bread   cheese   chicken   fish
> lamb   noodles   rice   vegetables

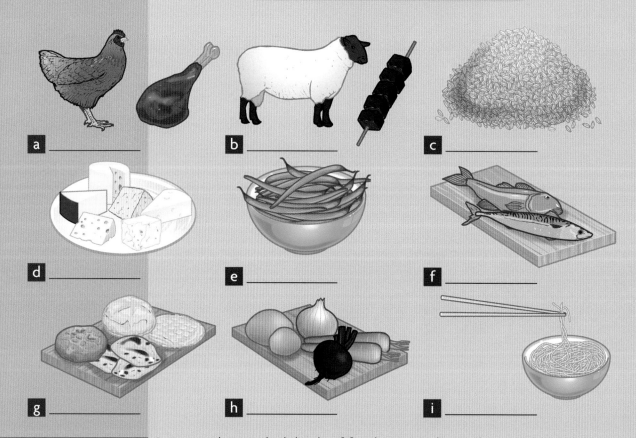

a _____

b _____

c _____

d _____

e _____

f _____

g _____

h _____

i _____

**2** Do you know which kinds of food are popular in China? Tick (✔) three kinds of food (a–i) that you think are popular in China.

# WHILE WATCHING

**3** ▶ Watch the video and circle all the words for food (a–i) you see and hear. How many kinds of food did you guess correctly?

**4** ▶ Watch again. Circle the correct answers.

1 Which Chinese city is in the video?
 a Shanghai
 b Beijing
 c Hong Kong
2 What is the most popular food in China?
 a rice
 b noodles
 c vegetables
3 How much of the world's rice comes from China?
 a a quarter ($\frac{1}{4}$)
 b a third ($\frac{1}{3}$)
 c a half ($\frac{1}{2}$)
4 How many years old are the fields in the video?
 a 300
 b 400
 c 500
5 What kind of meals are important in China?
 a meals with family
 b meals with friends
 c meals with business people

# DISCUSSION

**5** Work with a partner. Ask and answer the questions about your country.

1 What is the most popular food?
2 Do people like eating in restaurants or at home?
3 What kind of food do people eat at home?
4 Are rice dishes popular?
5 Are family meals important?

## PREPARING TO LISTEN

**1** You are going to listen to part of a lecture about food in cities. Before you listen, read the information below and answer the questions.

1 Which country is this text about?
2 What is the topic of the text?

# FACTS ABOUT FARMING

There are half a million farmers in the UK. This is about 1% of the population of the country.

Farmers grow fruit and vegetables and look after animals. They have to get up early to feed the chickens, cows and sheep. They sell milk, meat and other food to supermarkets in the cities.

Farmers are not rich. They have to spend money on their animals and on their farms. The supermarkets do not pay a lot of money for the food that they buy.

**2** Write the words in green next to the correct definitions.

1 _____ : the opposite of *poor*
2 _____ : food: apples, bananas, oranges, lemons, etc.
3 _____ : food: lamb, beef, chicken
4 _____ : to give money to somebody for something
5 _____ : to look after plants, flowers or food and then sell them
6 _____ : to give food to a person or animal
7 _____ : things that are true
8 _____ : all the people who live in a place, a city or a country
9 _____ : the number 1,000,000
10 _____ : 50% of something

# PRONUNCIATION FOR LISTENING

**3** 🔊 **8.1** Listen to and read these dialogues. Circle the numbers you hear.

  **1** **A:** Is the population there about *17 / 70* million?

      **B:** Um, no, I think it's about *17 / 70*.

      **A:** *17 / 70* million? OK, thanks.

  **2** **C:** We feed *16 / 60* children from poor families here.

      **D:** Sorry, how many children? *16 / 60*?

      **C:** No, *16 / 60*.

  **3** **E:** *13 / 30* % of this class are vegetarians – people who don't eat meat.

      **F:** *13 / 30*? Are you sure?

      **E:** No, no – *13 / 30*!

  **4** **G:** People in this city eat *15 / 50* thousand tonnes of beef every month.

      **H:** Is that true? *15 / 50* thousand tonnes every month?

      **G:** No, *15 / 50* thousand – not *15 / 50*.

## Pronunciation of *-teen* and *-ty* numbers

For *-teen* numbers (e.g. 13, 14, 15):

- stress the first syllable when the number is before a noun.

    *Fif-teen thousand tonnes every month?*
    *Se-ven-teen million?*

- stress the last syllable when the number is at the end of a statement.

    *Sorry, how many children? Six-teen?*      *No, no – thir-teen.*

For *-ty* numbers (e.g. 20, 30, 40), always stress the first syllable.

    *We feed six-ty children from poor families here.*      *No, six-ty.*

# WHILE LISTENING

**4** 🔊 **8.2** Listen to part of a lecture about food in cities. Are these statements true (T) or false (F)?

  **1** A lot of people grow fruit and vegetables in cities.

  **2** People in cities have more money than people in the country.

  **3** Food becomes expensive when people eat more meat.

  **4** Modern cities are bigger than before.

  **5** Today, more people live in the country than in cities.

**5** What is the main topic of the lecture? Circle the correct answer.

  **a** how to grow vegetables in a city

  **b** how to sell meat to people in cities

  **c** how to feed people in big cities

LISTENING FOR
DETAIL

UNLOCK
ONLINE

## Listening for numbers

You often hear facts in lectures. Many facts are about numbers.

*There are 100,000 science students in UK universities.*
*In Argentina, 97% of the population can read and write.*

6 🔊 8.2 Listen again. Write the number you hear next to the phrases.

1 _____ = important facts about cities

2 more than _____ % = money poor people spend on food

3 _____ = number of cities with 10 million people (today)

4 more than _____ = number of cities with 20 million people (in 2045)

5 _____ = fraction of people who live in cities (today)

6 _____ % = people who live in cities (in 2045)

7 Work with a partner. Compare answers. Use the phrases below to help you.

> What do you have for number ... ?

> I have ...

> What about you?

> I don't know the answer.

## DISCUSSION

8 Work in groups. Discuss the questions.

1 Do you live in the city or in the country?

2 Do you eat meat? Or are you a vegetarian?

3 What kind of meat do you eat?

4 Would you like to become a vegetarian? Why? / Why not?

# ◉ LANGUAGE DEVELOPMENT

## COUNTABLE AND UNCOUNTABLE NOUNS

UNLOCK ONLINE

EXPLANATION

### some/any/much/many

With countable and uncountable nouns, we can use *some* and *any*.

**countable**
(+) There are *some* apples.
(–) There are not *any* apples.
(?) Are there *any* apples?

**uncountable**
(+) There is *some* rice.
(–) There is not *any* rice.
(?) Is there *any* rice?

When we want to talk about numbers and measurements, we use *how many* and *how much*.

How many apples are there?        How much rice is there?

1  Look at the food nouns from this unit and write them in the correct column of the table below.

> apple  banana  beans  beef  bread  cheese
> chicken  fish  lamb  lemon  milk  noodles
> oranges  peppers  rice  vegetable

| countable nouns | uncountable nouns |
|---|---|
| apple | beef |
|  |  |

2  Correct the mistakes in the sentences.

1  There is some peppers on the plate.
2  There isn't some fish in the bowl.
3  How many rice is there?
4  There are any lemons on the table.
5  How much apples are there?

**3** Write the questions

1  A: _____?
   B: Yes, there are some bananas.
2  A: _____?
   B: There are three apples.
3  A: _____?
   B: No, there isn't any chicken.
4  A: _____?
   B: There is one bag of rice.
5  A: _____?
   B: There is one pepper.

## VOCABULARY FOR FOOD

**4** Work with a partner. Are the words in the box fast food (F), sweet food (S) or healthy food (H)?

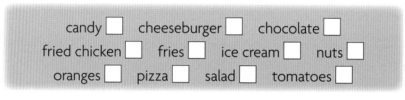

candy ☐   cheeseburger ☐   chocolate ☐
fried chicken ☐   fries ☐   ice cream ☐   nuts ☐
oranges ☐   pizza ☐   salad ☐   tomatoes ☐

**5** How many students in the class like each kind of food? Stand up and ask and answer questions. Use the phrases from the box to help you.

Do you like ... ? What about ... ?   What's your favourite food?
What food don't you like?   I like ... because ...
I don't like ... because ...

# LISTENING 2

## PREPARING TO LISTEN

**1** You are going to hear a student report the results of a survey. Before you listen, work with a partner. Take turns to ask and answer questions 1–4 in the slides.

## Question 1
**Where are you from?**

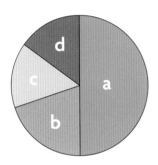

## Question 2
**Is food important in your culture?**

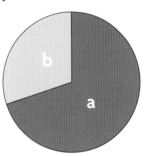

## Question 3
**Are family meals important?**

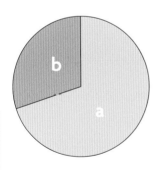

## Question 4
**Why are family meals (not) important?**

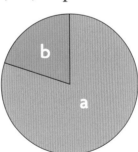

**2** Look at the four charts and answer the questions.

  **1** How many countries are you going to hear about in question 1?

  **2** Which answer do you think will be more popular to questions 2 and 3 – 'yes' or 'no'?

  **3** How many reasons are you going to hear about in question 4?

# WHILE LISTENING

**3** 🔊 **8.3** Listen to a student report the results of a survey and circle the correct answers.

1 The main topic of her survey is
   **a** food in Italy.      **b** food and culture.      **c** family meals.
2 Half the students come from
   **a** Italy.            **b** England.            **c** Egypt.
3 The student says that families are important in
   **a** Europe.          **b** Italy.              **c** culture.

**4** 🔊 **8.3** Listen again. Are these statements about the report true (T) or false (F)?

1 There were 30 students in the survey.
2 40% of students are from Spain.
3 Six students think food is not important in their culture.
4 Six students think family meals are important.
5 Many students think family meals are a good time to talk.
6 Some students think family meals are cheaper.

**5** 🔊 **8.3** Work with a partner. Use the words from the box to label the diagrams on page 149. Then listen again and check.

> a good time to talk    cheaper and healthier    Egypt
> England    Spain    Italy    yes (x2)    no (x2)

# DISCUSSION

**6** Work with a partner. Ask and answer the questions.

1 What are special holidays in your country?
2 Do you meet family for these special holidays?
3 Do people eat special food in these holidays? (What?)
4 Does the special food come from your country, or does it come from other countries? (Which ones?)
5 Do you agree with the student's statement: *Food is important in families, and families are important in culture*?

# CRITICAL THINKING

At the end of this unit, you are going to do the speaking task below.

Report the results of a survey.

## Use pie charts

The diagrams in Listening 2 (page 149) and below are pie charts. We can use pie charts to show different answers to the same question.

1  Read the text below. What is its topic?

2  Work with a partner. Take turns to ask and answer the questionnaire.

REMEMBER

## Questionnaire

The University wants to have an international food festival next month. We would like some information from you about this idea.

Q1  Would you like to have an international food festival?
Q2  Which countries would you like to come to the food festival?
Q3  Can you cook a dish from your country?
Q4  Would you like to cook a dish for the international food festival? (Which dishes?)

SOUTH  UNIVERSITY *of the*

3  Read the results of the survey of 100 students. Work in two groups.

**Group A:** Use the results to make pie charts for questions 1 and 2.
**Group B:** Use the results to make pie charts for questions 3 and 4.

APPLY

| Q1 | Yes: 75 | No: 25 | | |
|---|---|---|---|---|
| Q2 | China: 22 | Turkey: 19 | Saudi Arabia: 17 | |
| | Japan: 15 | Spain: 12 | Italy: 8 | France: 7 |
| Q3 | Yes: 60 | No: 40 | | |
| Q4 | fish and chips: 10 kabsah: 40 chicken and rice: 30 kebab: 20 | | | |

# SPEAKING

## PREPARATION FOR SPEAKING

### INTRODUCING A REPORT

**1** 🔊 **8.4** Sofia uses six statements to introduce her report. Number the sentences in the correct order (1–6). Then listen and check.

- [ ] My questions were on the topic of 'Food and culture'.
- [ ] This afternoon, I'm going to tell you about the results of my survey.
- [ ] There were 20 students in my survey.
- [ ] I'm Sofia.
- [ ] I think this is an interesting topic.
- [ ] Hello!

**2** 🔊 **8.5** Listen to two more introductions. Write the words and numbers from the box in the gaps below.

> 34   50   everybody   fast   good
> interesting   morning   traditional

---

Good (1)_____ ! I'm Tomoko. I'm going to tell you about the results of my survey. There were (2)_____ students in my survey. My topic was '(3)_____ Japanese food'. I think this is an (4)_____ topic.

---

Hello, (5)_____ ! I'm Ahmed. I'm going to tell you about the results of my survey. My topic was '(6)_____ food in Abu Dhabi'. There were (7)_____ students in my survey. I think this is a (8)_____ topic.

---

## PRONUNCIATION FOR SPEAKING

**3** 🔊 **8.6** Listen and repeat. Then listen again and underline the stress.

1 I'm go-ing to tell you a-bout the re-sults of my sur-vey.
2 There were fif-teen stu-dents in my sur-vey.
3 My to-pic was food and cul-ture.

### TALKING ABOUT THE RESULTS

**4** How many questions were there in Sofia's survey (Listening 2, page 149)?

**UNL⚙CK** LISTENING AND SPEAKING SKILLS 1

**5** 🔊 **8.7** Listen to eight statements from Sofia's report. Which statements are about

 a  the survey? 1_____

 b  the pie charts? 2_____

**6** 🔊 **8.7** Listen again. Write the correct phrases (a–h) in the gaps in the statements (1–8).

 a  My last question was
 b  my second question was
 c  interesting
 d  My third question was
 e  You can see here that
 f  to this question
 g  So you can see that
 h  my first question was

 1  OK, so, _____ 'Where are you from?'.
 2  _____ half of the students are from England.
 3  OK, _____ 'Is food important in your culture?'.
 4  The answers are _____ .
 5  _____ 'yes' is 70% and 'no' is 30%!
 6  _____ 'Are family meals important?'.
 7  _____ 'Why are family meals important?'.
 8  There were two answers _____ .

**7** Match the pairs.

 1  Question 1 was ...        a  My last question was ...
 2  Question 2 was ...        b  My second question was ...
 3  Question 3 was ...        c  My first question was ...
 4  Question 4 was ...        d  My third question was ...

**8** What phrase can we use to talk about pie charts? Write letters in the gaps.

 Y __ __   c __ __   s __ __   h __ __ __   t __ __ __ ...

**9** Work with a partner. Take turns to report on the international food festival (Critical thinking, page 151). Use the phrases on pages 152–153 to talk about:

a  the survey.
b  the pie charts.

*My first question was 'Would you like to have an international food festival?'. You can see here that 'yes' is 75% and 'no' is 25%.*

## SPEAKING TASK

For Exercises 10–13, work with a partner.

PREPARE

**1** Write your names in the questionnaire below.

**2** Choose a topic for your survey from the box. Add it to the questionnaire.

> fast food    sweet food    traditional food

---

Names:

Topic:

**Questions:**

Q1   Do you like … ?    YES ⦿   NO ⦿

Q2   What is your favourite kind of … ?

*Write the answers here:*

Q3   How often do you have … ?
  • Every day              ⦿
  • Every week             ⦿
  • Only on special holidays ⦿

Q4   Who do you usually eat with?
  • Your family            ⦿
  • Your friends           ⦿
  • On your own            ⦿

Number of students in survey:

---

**3** Interview students in your class.

- Ask questions 1–4 about your topic.
- Write the answers on the questionnaire.
- Write the number of students in your survey.

**4** Write your results in the table below. For question 2, write the kind of food and the number of people.

dates (5), ice cream (3), chocolate (1)

| Q1 | Yes: _____ No: _____ |
|---|---|
| Q2 | |
| Q3 | every day: _____ <br> every week: _____ <br> special holidays: _____ |
| Q4 | with family: _____ <br> with friends: _____ <br> on your own: _____ |

**5** Use the results to make a pie chart for each question.

**6** Practise your introduction (see Preparation for speaking, page 152).

**7** Write words and phrases that are true for you. Then practise your introduction.

Hello! I'm _____ (*name*) . This _____ (*time of day*), I'm going to tell you about the results of my survey. There were _____ (*number*) students in my survey. My topic was _____ (*topic*).

**8** Work in two groups. Report the results of your survey to your group.

| TASK CHECKLIST | ✔ |
|---|---|
| Did you do a survey on a topic about food? | |
| Did you report the results of your survey? | |
| Did you introduce your report? | |
| Did you use pie charts in your report? | |

## OBJECTIVES REVIEW

*I can ...*

understand a video about
food in China.

very                                              not very
well                                                well

listen for numbers.

very                                              not very
well                                                well

introduce a report.

very                                              not very
well                                                well

report the results of a
survey.

very                                              not very
well                                                well

# WORDLIST

| UNIT VOCABULARY | |
| --- | --- |
| apple (n) | lamb (n) |
| banana (n) | last (adv) |
| bean (n) | lemon (n) |
| beef (n) | meat (n) |
| bread (n) | milk (n) |
| cheese (n) | noodles (n) |
| chicken (n) | oranges (n) |
| fact (n) | pepper (n) |
| fast food (n) | pie chart (n) |
| feed (v) | poor (adj) |
| festival (n) | rice (n) |
| first (adv) | rich (adj) |
| fish (n) | second (adv) |
| fruit (n) | special (adj) |
| grow (v) | spend (v) |
| half (n) | sweet (n) |
| holiday (n) | third (adv) |
| international (adj) | vegetable (n) |

## LEARNING OBJECTIVES

| Watch and listen | Watch and understand a video about two animals in India |
| --- | --- |
| Listening skills | Listen for definitions |
| Speaking skills | Introduce a topic; use questions in a talk |
| Speaking task | Describe an animal |

## UNL🔒CK YOUR KNOWLEDGE

Work with a partner. Ask and answer the questions.

1 Which kind of animal can you see in the photograph?

2 Which country do you think the photograph shows?

3 How could you describe these animals?

4 Can you see animals like this in your country? What animals can you see in your country?

## PREPARING TO WATCH

**UNDERSTANDING KEY VOCABULARY**

**1** Label the picture with the words from the box.

> branch   eggs   flower   fruit   leaf/leaves

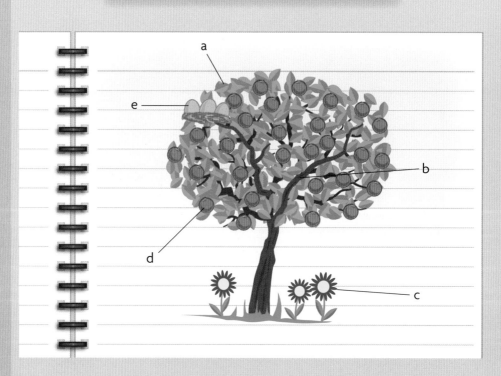

**2** Which animals live in forests? Make a list.

**3** Match the pairs of opposites.

| | | | |
|---|---|---|---|
| 1 | come down | a | look after |
| 2 | kill | b | buy |
| 3 | sell | c | leave |
| 4 | return | d | climb up |

**4** Write the words from the box next to the correct definition.

> government   horn   hunter   soldier

1 _____ *noun* [C] (GROUP) the group of people who control a country

2 _____ *noun* [C] a person or an animal that hunts animals for food or for sport

3 _____ *noun* [C or U] (ANIMAL) a long, hard bone that grows from the head or nose of an animal

4 _____ *noun* [C] a person who is in an army and wears a uniform

## WHILE WATCHING

**5** ▶ Watch the video and circle the correct answers.

1 Where do the animals in the video live?
   **a** China   **b** India   **c** Pakistan

2 Why are these two animals special?
   **a** Because they are very beautiful.
   **b** Because they are dangerous.
   **c** Because there are not many of them.

UNDERSTANDING MAIN IDEAS

**6** ▶ Watch again. Are the statements true (T) or false (F)?

1 There are only 2,000 red pandas in the world.     _____

2 Red pandas eat small animals.     _____

3 Some red pandas live in busy cities.     _____

4 Rhinos go to the river on hot days.     _____

5 There are only 3,000 rhinos in India.     _____

6 Soldiers kill rhinos for food.     _____

7 A rhino horn can sell for $100,000.     _____

8 Farmers look after red pandas and rhinos.     _____

UNDERSTANDING DETAIL

## DISCUSSION

**7** Work with a partner. Ask and answer the questions.

1 Should governments look after rare animals in their country?

2 Should governments stop hunters?

## PREPARING TO LISTEN

USING YOUR
KNOWLEDGE

**1** You are going to listen to two women talk about orangutans. Before you listen, work with a partner. What do you know about orangutans?

1 What do they look like? (Are they big animals?)
2 What do they eat?
3 Where do they live?

UNDERSTANDING
KEY VOCABULARY

**2** Label the photographs with words from the box.

hands   jungle   leaves   orangutan   stick   tree

**3** Complete these facts about orangutans with words from the box.

brain   climb   long   use   wet

1 They have very _____ arms.
2 They can _____ trees easily.
3 They like water, but they do not like getting _____ .
4 They _____ sticks to eat insects.
5 They have a big _____ .

## PRONUNCIATION FOR LISTENING

**4** Here are seven words from the recording. What kind of letters are in bold and red?

☐ ha**nds**      ☐ cli**mb**      ☐ wi**ld**      ☐ umb**r**ella
☐ brai**ns**      ☐ wor**ld**      ☐ grou**nd**

**5** 🔊 9.1 Listen to the seven words. Do we pronounce the letters in red? Write 'Y' for 'yes' or 'N' for 'no'.

EXPLANATION

## Silent consonants

We do not always pronounce every consonant when they are in a group.

friends (no 'd' sound)
sorry (only one 'r' sound)
where (no 'h' sound)
sticks (only one 'k' sound)

## WHILE LISTENING

**6** 🔊 **9.2** Listen to two women (Kate and Zaskia) talk about orangutans. In what order do you hear the information? Write numbers 1–4.

LISTENING FOR
MAIN IDEAS

☐ what orangutans eat
☐ what kind of places orangutans live in
☐ why orangutans are special
☐ what the name *orangutan* means

EXPLANATION

## Listening for definitions

Good speakers explain the meaning of new or difficult words. They give a definition of the words. We can use the words and phrases in red to define key vocabulary.

A falcon is a kind of bird.
Carnivore means an animal that eats meat.
It's a hunter. That means it kills other animals for food.
They are vegetarian, so they don't eat meat.

**7** 🔊 **9.2** Listen again. Then work with a partner. What do the words in bold mean?

LISTENING FOR
DETAIL

1 So *orangutan* means …
2 Orangutans are **arboreal**. That means …
3 They're **omnivores**, so …
4 A **primate** is a kind of …
5 They are good **toolmakers**. That means …

UNL⊘CK
ONLINE

**8** Match the words in Exercise 7 (1–5) to the correct definitions (a–e).

a … animal that can use its hands to climb trees.
b … they live in trees.
c … they can make things to help them.
d … 'the man in the forest'.
e … they can eat meat, fruit and vegetables.

## DISCUSSION

**9** Work with a partner. Read the sentences, then discuss the questions below.

Orangutans live only in Indonesia and Malaysia. They are special animals in these countries.

1 Which animals are special in your country? Why are they special?
2 Do you know any animals that are special in other countries?
   Russia – bear, Libya – lion, New Zealand – kiwi

# ⊙ LANGUAGE DEVELOPMENT

UNLOCK ONLINE

## VOCABULARY FOR ANIMALS

**1** Write the words from the box in the gaps in the diagram below.

cat   crocodile   horse   locust   snake   wasp

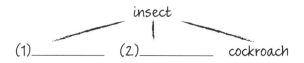

insect
(1)_____   (2)_____   cockroach

mammal
(3)_____   bear   (4)_____

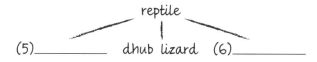

reptile
(5)_____   dhub lizard   (6)_____

### Group words

Try to learn new words in groups. A diagram is one way to do this.

**Note:** Words are often in more than one group.

Bears, lions and cats are mammals.
Bears and lions are hunters.
A lion is a kind of wild cat.
A whale and a fish are kinds of sea creature.

## DEFINITIONS

**2** Which phrase goes in the gap? Circle the correct answers.

1 A locust _____ insect.
   a is a kind of
   b is the name for

2 A horse is a mammal. _____ it has warm blood, and its babies are born alive, not eggs.
   a That means
   b means

3 Reptiles _____ animals with cold blood. For example, snakes are reptiles.
   a are
   b means

4 A 'herd' _____ a group of wild horses.
   a are
   b is the name for

5 Elephants have two big teeth _____ 'tusks'.
   a That means
   b called

**3** Read the texts. Which animals from Exercise 1 do they describe?

1

> This animal is a kind of reptile. They live in deserts in the Arab world. They live in 'burrows'. That means a hole in the ground. They eat plants and small insects.

2

> This animal is a kind of insect. They are small and yellow or green. They live in Africa, the Arab world and Asia. They travel in large groups called a 'swarm'. There are millions of these insects in each swarm.

**4** Choose an animal from Exercise 1. Use the phrases from the box to make a definition (don't say the animal's name).

> This animal is a kind of ...   They are *big / small*.
> They are *brown / green / white*.   They live in ...   They eat ...

**5** Work with a partner. Take turns to describe and guess animals from Exercise 1.

# LISTENING 2

## PREPARING TO LISTEN

**USING YOUR KNOWLEDGE**

**1** You are going to listen to two students talk about an animal from their country. Before you listen, which photographs show

1 a bald eagle?
2 an oryx?

**2** Work with a partner. Can you answer these questions?

1 Where do these animals live?
2 What do they eat?

**UNDERSTANDING KEY VOCABULARY**

**3** Write the words from the box in the correct column of the table below.

> cut   fish   grass   hard   jump   long
> rabbit   run   sharp

| nouns | verbs | adjectives |
|-------|-------|------------|
| fish  | cut   | hard       |
|       |       |            |

**4** Work with a partner. Take turns to ask and answer the questions. The answers are words from Exercise 3.

1 What should you do if you see a lion? *Run!*
2 Which animals live in the sea?
3 What do cows and sheep eat?
4 Which animal has long ears?
5 What can you do with a sharp knife?
6 What can kangaroos do very easily?
7 What is the opposite of *soft*?

## WHILE LISTENING

**5** 🔊 9.3 Listen to two students talk about an animal from their country. Number the photographs in the order you hear them (1–4).

LISTENING FOR MAIN IDEAS

**6** 🔊 9.3 Listen again and answer the questions.

LISTENING FOR DETAIL

### Jason

1 Which two countries can you see a bald eagle in?
2 What is a *nest*?
3 What do bald eagles eat?
4 What can bald eagles do with their beaks?

### Khaled

5 Can you see oryx in forests?
6 Where does Khaled come from?
7 What two things do oryx eat?
8 What does 'nomadic' mean?

UNLOCK ONLINE

**7** Label the photographs with these words.

beak   feathers   horns   nest

## DISCUSSION

**8** Work with a partner. Read the sentences, then discuss the questions below.

Governments pay people to look after bald eagles and oryx. If people do not look after these animals, they may die.

1 Is it important to look after wild animals?
2 Should governments pay people to look after animals?

# CRITICAL THINKING

At the end of this unit, you are going to do the speaking task below.

Describe an animal.

**1** Read the three texts below. Then answer the questions.

1 What kind of texts are a and c?
2 What kind of text is b?
3 Which kind of text do you use when you study English?
4 Which kind of text has more information?

**a**

❶                  Learner's dict ... ▼    **Search!**

## ❷ jump

UK 🔊   US 🔊   /dʒʌmp/   *verb*

### Definition

▸ to push your body up and away from the ground using your feet and legs:
❸ *They jumped into the water.*

**b**

## MyTranslator

From:    Choose language ▼

To:       English (UK)

**Translate!**

❹

**c**

## prey

❺ UK 🔊   US 🔊   /preɪ/   ❻ *noun [U]*

### Definition

▸ an animal that is hunted and killed by another animal
→ SEE ALSO ❼ bird of prey

**2** Match the numbers in the texts (1–7) to the phrases (a–g).

    **a** an example of the key word in a sentence

    **b** the search window

    **c** a collocation with the key word

    **d** the translation window

    **e** the key word

    **f** information about the grammar of the key word

    **g** the correct pronunciation of the key word

## Use online translation tools and dictionaries

Use online translation tools and dictionaries together.

From your language to English

1 Translate the name of an animal in your language into English.

2 Use an online dictionary to check the translation.

From English to your language

1 Find the definition of the word in an online dictionary.

2 Use an online translation tool to check that you understand the word and the definition.

**3** Use an online translation tool and a dictionary to write the names of the animals below.

    **1** What are these animals in English?

    **2** What are the baby animals called?

mothers and baby animals

# SPEAKING

## PREPARATION FOR SPEAKING

### INTRODUCING A TOPIC

1 🔊 9.4 Listen to the beginning of Jason and Khaled's presentations about animals again. Write the missing words in the gaps.

1 OK, good morning! I'm Jason, and <sup>(1)</sup> t_____ I'm going to <sup>(2)</sup> t_____ you <sup>(3)</sup> a_____ a bird from my country – the American bald eagle.

2 OK, good morning <sup>(4)</sup> e_____ . My name's Khaled and I'm going to <sup>(5)</sup> t_____ <sup>(6)</sup> a_____ the animal in <sup>(7)</sup> t_____ photograph <sup>(8)</sup> h_____ . So this is an Arabian oryx.

2 Use the words from the box to check your answers to Exercise 1.

> about (x2)   everybody   here   talk   tell   this   today

### USING QUESTIONS IN A TALK

> ## Using questions
> You can ask and answer your own questions in a talk to help your listeners understand you.

3 🔊 9.5 Listen to three parts of Jason's talk. Which question below (a–c) goes in each gap?

1 _____ Well, you can see them in the US and Canada and here's a photograph of one.

2 Some nests can be very big. _____ Well, there was one eagle's nest that was more than 1,000 kilos!

3 _____ Well, fish are their prey. That means the eagles hunt them.

a How big can they be?
b So what do bald eagles eat?
c OK, so where do they live?

UNL⊘CK LISTENING AND SPEAKING SKILLS 1

**4** Read part of a student's talk below about brown bears and match the questions (1–5) to the gaps.

   **1** How do they live?
   **2** what do they eat?
   **3** why are they special?
   **4** where do these bears live?
   **5** where can you see brown bears?

OK, hello, everybody. My name's Luo Yan, and I'm going to talk about brown bears. This is a photograph of a brown bear.

So, (a)_____ Well, they live in forests and near rivers. They often live in mountains.

And (b)_____ In a lot of countries! Brown bears live in America and Europe and parts of Asia.

(c)_____ Well, they sleep for the winter and they hunt in the summer. They have to eat a lot in the summer, so bears are often hungry.

And so (d)_____ Well, they eat a lot of different things. They like fruit, fish, vegetables, nuts and grass.

So (e)_____ Well, they are very, very strong animals. They can move rocks and trees and other big things easily.

**5** 🔊 9.6 Listen and check your answers.

**6** Read Luo Yan's talk again.

   **1** What word often comes before a question?
   **2** What word often comes before the answer to a question?

## PRONUNCIATION FOR SPEAKING

### Pauses

You can also use pauses in a talk to help your listeners to understand you.

**7** 🔊 9.6 Listen again and read the audio script. Indicate where there is a pause between words.

OK, // hello, everybody. // My name's Luo Yan, // and I'm going to talk about // brown bears. // This is a photograph of a brown bear.

## SPEAKING TASK

**1** Work in three groups: A, B and C. Read a text about an animal.

Group A (tigers): Turn to page 194.
Group B (ants): Turn to page 196.
Group C (koalas): Turn to page 198.

**2** Find these key words in your text and check the meaning.

| Group A | Group B | Group C |
|---|---|---|
| tigers | ants | koalas |
| 1 climate (n) | 1 wing (n) | 1 fur (n) |
| 2 predator (n) | 2 leaves (pl n) | 2 waterproof (adj) |
| 3 dark (n) | 3 lung (n) | 3 pouch (n) |
| 4 stripe (n) | 4 breathe (v) | 4 joey (n) |

**3** Work with your group and write definitions for your four words in Exercise 2. Use an online dictionary to help you (see Critical thinking, page 168).

**4** Take turns to ask and answer questions about your animals.

1 Where do they live?
2 What do they eat?
3 How do they live?
4 Why are they special?

**5** Use the internet to find photographs of your animal. Look for photographs that can help you explain your new words.

**6** Write words and phrases in the gaps that are true for you.

OK, hello, everybody. My name's _____ (*your name*) and I'm going to talk about _____ (*your animal, plural*). This is a photograph of (a/an) _____ (*your animal, singular*).

**7** Work with a partner in your group. Take turns to practise your introductions.

UNL**O**CK LISTENING AND SPEAKING SKILLS 1

**8** Work in groups of three: Student A, Student B and Student C.
Take turns to

- describe your animal and explain the four key words.
- listen and answer the questions in the table.

| animal (*tigers/ants/koalas*) | |
|---|---|
| 1 Where do they live? | |
| 2 What do they eat? | |
| 3 How do they live? | |
| 4 Why are they special? | |

**9** Return to your group: A, B or C.

1 Compare your tables from Exercise 8. Do you have the same answers?
2 Look at the words for the other two groups in Exercise 2. Do you know what they mean?

**10** Check your answers with the class.

**11** Which animals are the most interesting? Tigers, ants or koalas?

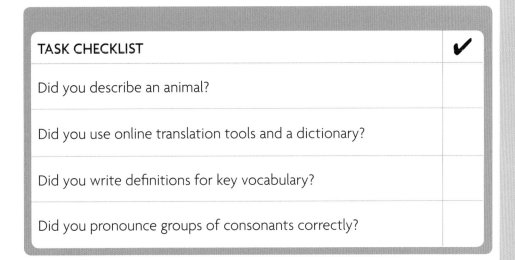

| TASK CHECKLIST | ✔ |
|---|---|
| Did you describe an animal? | |
| Did you use online translation tools and a dictionary? | |
| Did you write definitions for key vocabulary? | |
| Did you pronounce groups of consonants correctly? | |

## OBJECTIVES REVIEW

*I can ...*

understand a video about
two animals in India.

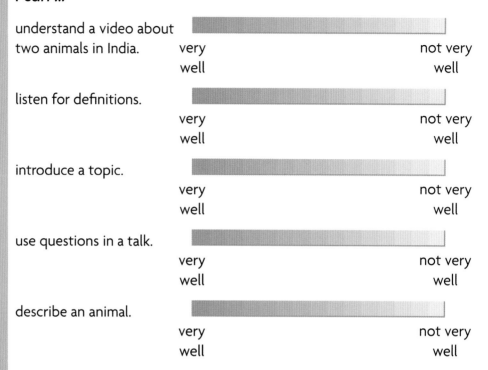

very
well

not very
well

listen for definitions.

very
well

not very
well

introduce a topic.

very
well

not very
well

use questions in a talk.

very
well

not very
well

describe an animal.

very
well

not very
well

# WORDLIST

| UNIT VOCABULARY | |
|---|---|
| angry (adj) | kangaroo (n) |
| beak (n) | long (adj) |
| brain (n) | nest (n) |
| camel (n) | orangutan (n) |
| climb (v) | rabbit (n) |
| cup (n) | race (n) |
| cut (v) | road sign (n) |
| feather (n) | sharp (adj) |
| grass (n) | stick (n) |
| hand (n) | tired (adj) |
| horn (n) | wet (adj) |
| jump (v) | wild (adj) |
| jungle (n) | |

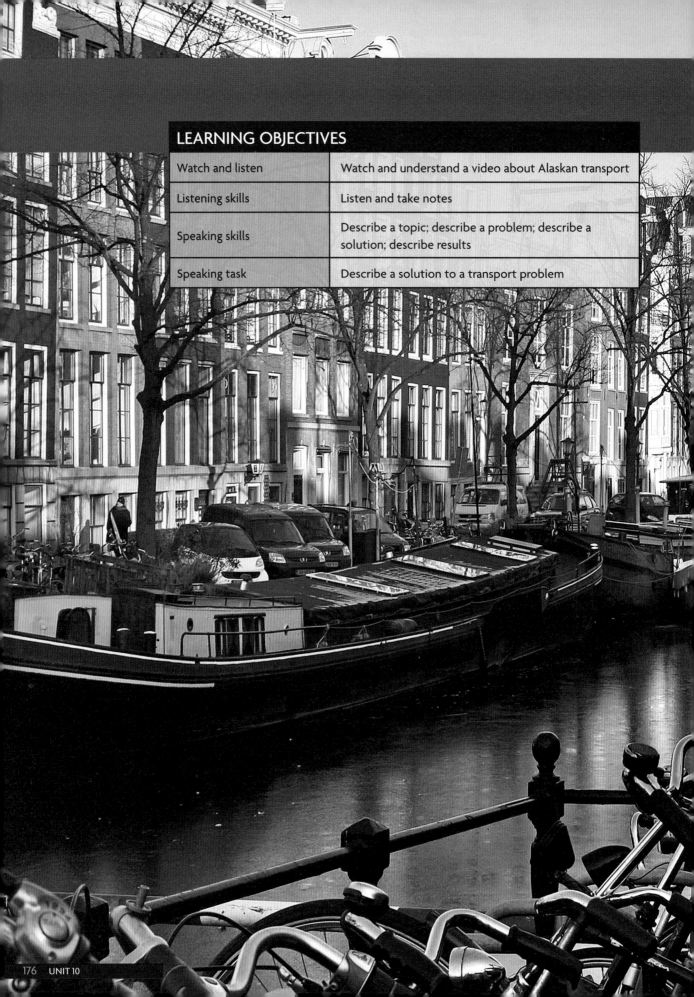

## LEARNING OBJECTIVES

| | |
|---|---|
| Watch and listen | Watch and understand a video about Alaskan transport |
| Listening skills | Listen and take notes |
| Speaking skills | Describe a topic; describe a problem; describe a solution; describe results |
| Speaking task | Describe a solution to a transport problem |

## UNL⌀CK YOUR KNOWLEDGE

Work with a partner. Ask and answer the questions.

1 Which country do you think is shown in the photograph? (How do you know?)

2 Which forms of transport in the photograph
   a are more modern?
   b did people use in the past?

3 Is there a problem with traffic in your city?

## PREPARING TO WATCH

**1** You are going to watch a video about Alaskan transport. Before you listen, which forms of transport can you see in the photographs from the video?

> boat   dog sled   hovercraft   plane   snowmobile   train

**2** Work with a partner. Look at the map and read the information below. Then answer the underlined question.

You are in Alaska. It is winter. It is very cold and there is a lot of snow and [1]**ice**. You have to take [2]**supplies** 50 km from the city to a small town. There are no [3]**roads** to the town. Which form of transport do you think is best? Why?

[1] **ice:** the hard form of water when it is very cold
[2] **supplies:** food, tools and other useful things people need to live
[3] **road:** the place where cars and other transport can drive

**3** Are the statements true (T) or false (F)? (Check the meaning of the words in bold to help you.)

1 Ice is **frozen** water. _____
2 It is safe to **stand** on **thin** ice. _____
3 When ice is **thick**, it is very easy to **break**. _____
4 Your umbrella is **useless** if there is a big **hole** in it. _____

## WHILE WATCHING

**4** ▶ Watch the video and answer the questions.

1 What is the weather like in Alaska in winter?
2 What happens to the rivers?
3 Which forms of transport do people use in winter?
4 Why can't they use
  a cars?
  b boats or planes?

**5** Are the statements true (T) or false (F)?

1 The video is about Alaska in the winter. _____
2 Some frozen rivers are very thin and less than 5 cm. _____
3 A dog walks on the river to test the ice. _____
4 A tractor can fall through thin ice. _____
5 A dog sled takes a lot of supplies to the small town of Akiachak. _____
6 A hovercraft falls through the ice. _____

**6** Work with a partner. Compare your answers.

**7** ▶ Watch again. Check your answers.

## DISCUSSION

**8** Work with a partner. Which forms of transport do you think are best in these places? Use the phrases in the box below to help you.

1 a desert
2 a mountain
3 a group of islands in the sea
4 a jungle

What about ... ?　　I think ... is better. What do you think?
Yes, I agree.　　I'm not sure. I think ... is better.

# LISTENING 1

## PREPARING TO LISTEN

**1** You are going to listen to a man called Steve Miller talk about Transport for London. Before you listen, decide if the forms of transport in the box are private or public. Write them in the correct column of the table below.

> bicycle    bus    car    ferry    motorbike
> river taxi    taxi    train    tram    underground

| private | public |
|---|---|
|  |  |
|  |  |

**2** Which forms of transport do you think are in London?

**3** Circle the correct word in each sentence.

1 Excuse me! How much is a train *journey* / *passenger* / *ticket* to Liverpool?
2 Hi! How was your *journey* / *passenger* / *ticket* to London?
3 I had a conversation with an interesting *journey* / *passenger* / *ticket* on the ferry.

## PRONUNCIATION FOR LISTENING

**4** 🔊 10.1 Look at the years. Listen and repeat.

> 1238    1868    1923    1996    2005    2015

**5** 🔊 10.2 Listen and write the years.

1 _____
2 _____
3 _____
4 _____
5 _____

**6** What do you notice about the last number in Exercise 5?

EXPLANATION

## Pronouncing years

Pronounce years in two parts with *and* or two parts only.

| | |
|---|---|
| 1994 | [nineteen] [ninety-four] |
| 1238 | [twelve] [thirty-eight] |
| 570 | [five hundred] and [seventy] |
| 2005 | [two thousand] and [five] |
| 2015 | [two thousand] and [fifteen] or [twenty fifteen] |

a

b

Steve Miller works for Transport for London (TfL).

c

Many Londoners use Oyster cards.

d

**7** Work with a partner. What can you see in the photographs?

**8** Which do you think Steve is going to discuss?

PREDICTING
CONTENT USING
VISUALS

## WHILE LISTENING

### Listening and taking notes

When you listen to a talk, take notes. Write the

- key words.
- numbers.

Then compare your notes with a partner.

LISTENING FOR
MAIN IDEAS

**9** 🔊 **10.3** Listen to Steve Miller talk about Transport for London and take notes.

**10** Work with a partner. Use your notes to ask and answer the questions.

1 What is the topic of his talk?
2 What does Transport for London (TfL) do?
3 How many people travel in London?
4 When did the London Underground open?
5 What is an Oyster card?

LISTENING FOR
DETAIL

**11** 🔊 **10.3** Listen again and answer the questions.

1 Which five forms of transport does Steve talk about?
- <u>London Underground</u>
- _____
- _____
- _____
- _____

2 How old is the London Underground? _____
3 What year did TfL introduce Oyster cards? _____
4 Why did TfL need Oyster cards? _____
5 How can people pay for their journeys with an Oyster card?

_____

## DISCUSSION

**12** Work with a partner. Ask and answer the questions.

1 Do you live in a busy city? If not, have you visited one? Do you like it?
2 Which forms of transport do you use? What do you use them for?
3 Which form of transport do you use most often? Why?

# ⊙ LANGUAGE DEVELOPMENT

## VOCABULARY FOR TRANSPORT

UNL⊙CK
ONLINE

1 Match the verbs (1–10) to the definitions (a–j).

| | | | |
|---|---|---|---|
| 1 | ride | a | arrange to have a seat on a plane, train, bus |
| 2 | take | b | begin to fly |
| 3 | go by | c | get on a bus, train, plane or boat |
| 4 | depart | d | get to a place |
| 5 | arrive | e | leave a place |
| 6 | board | f | move or travel somewhere |
| 7 | reserve | g | show your ticket at an airport |
| 8 | check in | h | the action of a plane arriving on the ground after flying |
| 9 | take off | i | travel on a bicycle or motorbike |
| 10 | land | j | travel somewhere by using a bus, train, car |

2 Write the correct form of the verbs from Exercise 1 in the gaps.

1 Can you _____ a motorbike?

2 You can _____ a seat on a train.

3 The train _____ at platform 1.

4 The plane _____ from London at 11.00.

5 Do you like to _____ by train?

6 You must _____ the boat – it's going to depart!

7 Do you _____ the bus to school?

8 You must show your ticket and your passport when you _____ at the airport.

9 I don't like flying, especially at the start when the plane _____ .

10 I feel happy at the end of the flight when the plane _____ .

## THE PAST SIMPLE

EXPLANATION

### Past simple: positive

We use the past simple to talk about an event or an activity in the past.

The London Underground opened in 1863.
Fewer people lived and worked in London.
In 2003, we introduced the Oyster card.
We wanted a better kind of ticket.
We needed a faster ticket system.

We add -ed to regular verbs in the past, or just -d to verbs that end in -e.

(See Pronunciation for speaking, page 190)

## Past simple: irregular verbs

Some verbs are irregular. They do not add -d/-ed in the past simple. Learn irregular past forms.

**3** Write the correct infinitive form next to these irregular past simple verbs.

1  _be_ → was/were
2  _do_ → did
3  _have_ → had
4  _____ → made
5  _____ → took

6  _____ → could
7  _____ → put
8  _____ → went
9  _____ → came

**4** Write the verbs (in brackets) in the past simple.

1  No, I _____ (take) a taxi.
2  He _____ (go) to the train station.
3  She _____ (have) a good journey.
4  No, it _____ (be) too far for bicycles.
5  She _____ (walk) home.

**5** Match the sentences from Exercise 4 (1–5) to a–e.

a  Mika didn't have a problem on the train. _____3_____
b  Fatima couldn't find a taxi, so ... _____
c  Did you take the train? _____
d  Faisal didn't go to the airport. _____
e  Could they ride their bicycles? _____

**6** Look at a–e in Exercise 5.

1  Circle the verbs in negative statements.
2  Underline the verbs in questions.

**7** Look at your answers to Exercise 6. Write the correct words in the gaps.

1  Use _____ + the infinitive in negative statements.
2  Use _____ + subject + the infinitive in questions.

**8** Work with a partner. Take turns to ask and answer the questions. Remember to use *did* in the questions.

| Last week, | | | |
|---|---|---|---|
| 1 _____ you take a bus? | | Where _____ you go? | I went to the university. |
| 2 _____ you go by car? | Yes, I did. / No, I didn't. | | |
| 3 _____ you take a plane? | | | |
| 4 _____ you travel by boat? | | What _____ you do there? | I studied in the library. |
| 5 _____ you ride a bicycle? | | | |

# LISTENING 2

## PREPARING TO LISTEN

**1** You are going to listen to somebody describe a solution to a transport problem. Before you listen, look at the photographs (1–6) and match them to the words in the box.

> metro railway   sky bridge   sky train
> traffic jam   travelator

**2** Discuss the questions with a partner.

1 Which of these things do you have in your country?
2 Which are problems, and which are solutions?

**3** Write the transport words and phrases in the box in the phrases and sentences below. Use the glossary at the back of the book to check meanings.

> commuters   congestion   destination
> get stuck   transport system

1 The government is working hard to improve the _____ .
2 _____ in traffic jams
3 _____ have to drive to metro stations.
4 It takes a long time to get to your _____ .
5 Public transport reduces _____ .

## WHILE LISTENING

**4** 🔊 **10.4** Listen to somebody describe a solution to a transport problem and write notes. Then compare your notes with a partner.

> *Topic:*
> (1)_____
>
> *Facts:*
> *Cities are* (2)_____ . *Petrol is* (3)_____ *and causes*
> (4)_____ .
>
> *Public transport is good because* (5)_____ .
> *Problems with buses:*
> (6)_____
>
> *Problems with the metro system:*
> (7)_____
>
> *Solutions:*
> *make the metro system bigger by going* (8)_____
> *go over the city with* (9)_____
> *Reason:*
> *people won't need to* (10)_____

**5** Answer the questions. Use your notes to help you.

1 Why are cities congested?
2 What are the problems with cars?
3 What do some countries say is a good idea?
4 Which place is working hard to improve the transport system?
5 What is the plan in Dubai?
6 What other cities does Iman speak about?

**6** 🔊 **10.4** Listen again, take more notes if you need to and check your answers.

## DISCUSSION

**7** Work with a partner. Discuss the questions.

1 Do you like using the types of transport Iman spoke about? Why? / Why not?
2 Do you agree with Iman that
   a cars are a problem? Why? / Why not?
   b public transport is a good solution? Why? / Why not?

# CRITICAL THINKING

At the end of this unit, you are going to do the speaking task below.

Describe a solution to a transport problem.

**1** Below are Iman's notes for her talk about transport in cities. Match the words in the box to the correct part of her notes (1–4).

problem   solution   topic   result

1 _____
Public transport is good. It reduces:
· congestion.
· pollution.

2 _____
Cars:
· use a lot of petrol.
· can be dangerous.

3 _____
Public transport improvements:
· Introduce more buses and bus routes.
· Make the metro system bigger.
· Build sky bridges and travelators to connect stations.

4 _____
People:
· can walk around easily.
· won't need to drive.

## Use flow charts

Use notes to help you talk about a topic. Put your notes into a flow chart. A flow chart can help you organize your ideas.

**2** Work with a partner. Match the pairs.

1 topic
2 problem
3 solution
4 result

a Drivers on Road 56 went very fast – there were a lot of accidents.
b More traffic police started to travel on Road 56. They watched the road with cameras.
c There are not as many accidents now. Road 56 is safer.
d Is Road 56 safe for drivers?

**3** Make a flow chart on the topic of Road 56.

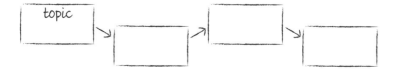

topic

**4** Work with a partner. Take turns to talk about Road 56. Use your flow charts to help you.

# SPEAKING

## PREPARATION FOR SPEAKING

**1** Look at the photographs of a river. What was the problem before?

Before

After

**2** On the next page are some notes for a talk on this topic. Match the questions (1–4) to the correct notes (a–d).

1 What is the topic?
2 What was the problem?
3 What was the solution?
4 Was it a good solution? (What was the result?)

*a*
- *Petrol from old ships killed the fish.*
- *Fishermen were angry because there were no fish in the rivers.*

*b*
- *More companies send goods\* by river today.*
- *More ships can make rivers dirty.*

*c*
- *The rivers are cleaner and there are more fish than before.*
- *The companies were not happy because modern ships are expensive.*

*d*
- *Companies have to pay to clean the river.*
- *Companies have to use modern ships.*

\* goods (n): things that companies make and sell

**3** Make a flow chart for this talk with four parts. Use the information in Exercise 2 to make notes.

## DESCRIBING A TOPIC

**4** 🔊 **10.5** Listen to Iman again. Then write the words and phrases from the box in the gaps below.

> can be   For example   population
> This is because   This means that

The (1)_____ of cities grows more quickly than in the countryside. (2)_____ cities become really congested. (3)_____ everyone uses cars to travel around the city, and this (4)_____ a problem. (5)_____, it takes a long time to get to your destination, so drivers need to use a lot of petrol ...

**5** 🔊 **10.6** Write write the words and phrases from the box in the gaps below. Then listen to Anna and check your answers.

> become dirty   For example   sending goods   ships   Ships

(1)_____ are great for (2)_____ by river. Ships are cheaper and often cleaner than road transport. But (3)_____ have some problems. (4)_____, when there are a lot of ships, rivers can (5)_____ .

**6** How can you finish the sentences about trains? Discuss your ideas in class.

- Trains are great for ...
- They are ... / We can ...
- But trains have some problems. For example, ...

## DESCRIBING A PROBLEM

**7** 🔊 **10.7** Write the verbs (in brackets) in the past simple. Then listen to Anna and check your answers.

You can see in this photograph that this <sup>(1)</sup>_____ (*happen*) in Europe. A lot of companies <sup>(2)</sup>_____ (*use*) old ships. Old ships <sup>(3)</sup>_____ (*be*) cheaper, but they <sup>(4)</sup>_____ (*have*) some problems. For example, petrol <sup>(5)</sup>_____ (*come*) out of the ships and into the rivers. The petrol <sup>(6)</sup>_____ (*kill*) the fish. Fishermen <sup>(7)</sup>_____ (*be*) angry because they <sup>(8)</sup>_____ (*cannot*) catch any fish.

## PRONUNCIATION FOR SPEAKING

**8** 🔊 **10.8** Listen and repeat the verbs in the past tense.

happened _____    used _____    visited _____    guessed _____
added _____    hated _____    asked _____    helped _____
showed _____    watched _____    changed _____    decided

**9** 🔊 **10.8** Listen again. What sound do you hear at the end of each verb? Write /t/, /d/ or /ɪd/ beside each verb in Exercise 8.

**10** Write the correct heading – /t/, /d/ or /ɪd/ – in the table.

| Prounciation of -*d/-ed* in regular past simple verbs | | |
|---|---|---|
| Past simple verb pronounced<br>1 _____ | Past simple verb pronounced<br>2 _____ | Past simple verb pronounced<br>3 _____ |
| When a verb ends in these sounds:<br><br>stop /p/<br>laugh /f/<br>miss /s/<br>like /k/<br>finish /ʃ/<br>watch /tʃ/ | When a verb ends with a vowel sound or these consonant sounds:<br><br>grab /b/<br>jog /g/<br>save /v/<br>buzz /z/<br>massage /ʒ/<br>change /dʒ/<br>climb /m/<br>listen /n/<br>ring /ŋ/<br>travel /l/<br>breathe /ð/ | When a regular verb ends with a /t/ or /d/ sound:<br><br>visit /t/<br>decide /d/ |

## DESCRIBING A SOLUTION

**11** Put the words and phrases in order to make statements.

1 the / to make / They / rivers / companies / decided / clean / .
2 modern / ships / The / buy / companies / had to / .
3 cleaned / the / rivers / companies / The / .

**12** Work with a partner. Discuss the questions in class.

1 What problems do trains have in cities?
2 What solutions do you know for those problems?

## DESCRIBING RESULTS

**13** 🔊 10.9 Listen and number the statements in the correct order.

☐ Why? Because the companies weren't happy that they had to clean the rivers.
☐ I think it was a good solution.
☐ But there was some good news.
☐ That means there are more fish than before.
☐ So, was it a good solution? Well, that's a very interesting question!
☐ And they didn't want to pay to clean the rivers.
☐ The fishermen are happier because the rivers are cleaner.
☐ The old ships were cheap, but modern ships are expensive.

**14** Work with a partner. Take turns to describe the result in Exercise 13. Use the phrases in the box to help you.

I think it was a good solution.

I don't think it was a good solution.

Why? Because …

That means …

## SPEAKING TASK

Work in two groups, A and B.

**1** You are going to describe a transport problem and then talk about the solution. First, discuss the questions.

    **1** Are traffic jams a problem in your city/country?
    **2** Why are traffic jams bad for
       **a** business?
       **b** family life?

**PREPARE**

**2** Work with a partner in your group.

Group A:  Turn to page 195.
Group B:  Turn to page 197.

**3** Use a flow chart to plan your talk (see Critical thinking, page 187).

    **1** Make a flow chart with four parts.
    **2** Use the information about your city (Paris or Melbourne) to make notes.

**PRESENT**

**4** Work with a partner from your group. Take turns to practise your talk.

    **1** Describe
       • the topic.        • the solution.
       • the problem.      • the result.
    **2** Use your notes and the photographs of the city to help you.

**5** Work with a partner from the other group. Take turns to describe the solution to the transport problem in Paris or Melbourne.

**DISCUSS**

**6** Discuss the questions in class.

    **1** Which city had the best solution?
    **2** Is that solution a good idea for your city/country? Why? / Why not?

| TASK CHECKLIST | ✔ |
| --- | --- |
| Did you describe a solution to a transport problem? | |
| Did you use a flow chart to plan your talk? | |
| Did you use past simple verbs? | |
| Did you pronounce regular past simple verbs with /t/, /d/ and /ɪd/? | |

## OBJECTIVES REVIEW

*I can ...*

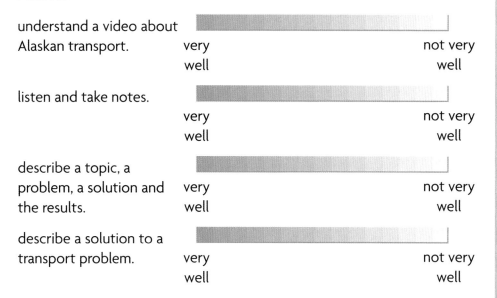

understand a video about Alaskan transport.

very well          not very well

listen and take notes.

very well          not very well

describe a topic, a problem, a solution and the results.

very well          not very well

describe a solution to a transport problem.

very well          not very well

## WORDLIST

| UNIT VOCABULARY | | |
|---|---|---|
| accident (n) | frozen (adj) | ride (v) |
| air-conditioned (adj) | get stuck (v) | river taxi (n) |
| arrive (v) | goods (n) | road rage (n) |
| bicycle (n) | hole (n) | sky train (n) |
| board (v) | ice (n) | solution (n) |
| boat (n) | introduce (v) | stand (v) |
| break (v) | journey (n) | taxi (n) |
| bus (n) | land (v) | ticket (n) |
| car (n) | metro railway (n) | traffic (n) |
| check in (v) | motorbike (n) | traffic jam (n) |
| commuter (n) | need (v) | train (n) |
| congestion (n) | passenger (n) | tram (n) |
| depart (v) | petrol (n) | transport system (n) |
| destination (n) | plane (n) | travelator (n) |
| ferry (n) | private (adj) | the underground (n) |
| flight (n) | public (adj) | useless (adj) |
| fly (v) | reserve (v) | |

# PAIRWORK ACTIVITIES

## UNIT 1: PEOPLE, SPEAKING, EXERCISE 1

### Student A

Spell the words for your partner.

1 M–E–X–I–C–A–N
2 O–M–A–N–I
3 E–G–Y–P–T–I–A–N

## UNIT 4: PLACES, SPEAKING, EXERCISES 1, 2 AND 4

### Group A (Student A)

1 You are going to do a role-play with Group B. Before the role-play, look at the map below. Work with other students from Group A and practise giving directions from the fountain to the places (1–5).

   1 the bank
   2 the Language Centre
   3 the Physics building
   4 the History building
   5 the supermarket

2 Student B will ask you for directions.

## UNIT 9, ANIMALS, SPEAKING, EXERCISE 1

### Group A

### Tigers

Tigers live in jungles and forests. You can find them in India, China and countries in South-East Asia. They can live in hot and cold climates.

Tigers are bigger than other wild cats. They are predators. They can see in the dark and so they usually hunt at night.

Tigers are orange, white and black and they are famous for their stripes. Every tiger's stripes are different.

### The University of Alpha

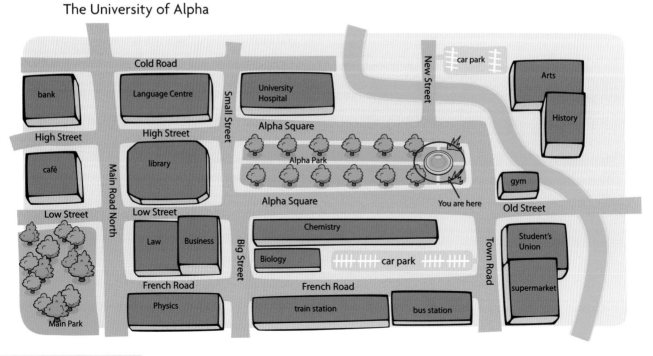

# UNIT 1: PEOPLE, LISTENING 2, EXERCISE 6

## Student A

Ask Student B these questions about the person in photograph b on page 23.

> *What's her name?*
> *Where's she from?*
> *Why is she famous?*
> *Who are her parents?*

Read this information. Then answer Student B's questions about the person in photograph e on page 23.

> Name:        *Kobe Bryant*
> Country:     *the United States*
> Occupation:  *basketball player*
> Parents:     *father – Joe Bryant, a*
>              *famous basketball player*
>              *mother – Pam Bryant*

# UNIT 6: JOBS, LISTENING 2, EXERCISE 2

## Student A

**About you**

My name's Alan Green and I'm from Portland, USA. I'm a student here at the University of Yukon. I would like to work at the Sports Centre after my degree.

I'm fit and strong and I love sport. I can speak English and French.

My favourite sports are football and basketball. I can also teach karate and judo.

# UNIT 10, TRANSPORT, SPEAKING, EXERCISE 2

## Group A
## Paris, France

Look at the photographs of traffic in Paris. Then match the questions below (1–4) to the correct notes (a–d).

**Before**

**After**

1  What is the topic?
2  What was the problem?
3  What was the solution?
4  Was it a good solution? (What was the result?)

a • There were a lot of traffic jams.
  • People didn't like them.
b • Yes! People love it. It is easier to travel in the city.
  • Many cities want to use the same solution, e.g. London and New York.
c • More people have cars today.
  • There are more problems with traffic in cities.
d • Make new roads for buses.
  • Make new roads for bicycles.

# UNIT 1: PEOPLE, SPEAKING, EXERCISE 1

## Student B

Spell the words for your partner.

4 E–M–I–R–A–T–I
5 J–A–P–A–N–E–S–E
6 T–U–R–K–I–S–H

# UNIT 4: PLACES, SPEAKING, EXERCISES 1, 3 AND 4

## Group B (Student B)

1 You are going to do a role-play with Group A. Before the role-play, look at the map below. Work with other students from Group B and practise giving directions from the statue to the places (1–5).

1 the History building
2 the train station
3 the Physics building
4 the bus station
5 the gym

2 Student A will ask you for directions.

# UNIT 9, ANIMALS, SPEAKING, EXERCISE 1

## Group B

### Ants

There are more than 12,000 different kinds of ant. You can find ants in many different countries all over the world.

Ants live together in groups. In each group, there are workers and a queen. The queen ant has wings.

Ants are very strong. For example, they can carry food and leaves that are bigger than their bodies. They don't have lungs. They breathe through their bodies.

Ants eat many different kinds of food. For example, they eat fruit and vegetables.

## The University of Beta

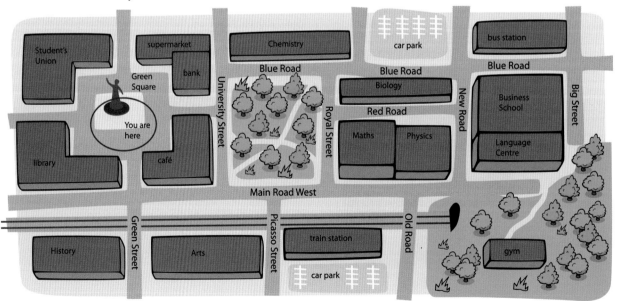

## UNIT 1: PEOPLE, LISTENING 2, EXERCISE 6

### Student B

Read this information. Then answer Student A's questions about the person in photograph b on page 23.

| | |
|---|---|
| *Name:* | *Victoria Beckham* |
| *Country:* | *the United Kingdom* |
| *Occupation:* | *fashion designer* |
| *Parents:* | *father – Anthony Adams* |
| | *mother – Doreen Adams* |

Ask Student A these questions about the person in photograph e on page 23.

*What's his name?*
*Where's he from?*
*Why is he famous?*
*Who are his parents?*

## UNIT 6: JOBS, LISTENING 2, EXERCISE 2

### Student B

**About you**

I'm Lucy Lau and I'm from Vancouver, Canada. I speak English, French and Cantonese. I have a degree in Sports Science.

In Vancouver, I teach zumba, pilates and yoga. I'm also a good tennis player. I think it is important to be a kind and polite. A fitness instructor should help people.

I would like to work with you.

## UNIT 10: TRANSPORT, SPEAKING, EXERCISE 2

### Group B

**Melbourne, Australia**

Look at the photographs of traffic in Melbourne. Then match the questions below (1–4) to the correct notes (a–d).

Before

After

1. What is the topic?
2. What was the problem?
3. What was the solution?
4. Was it a good solution? (What was the result?)

a • There were a lot of traffic jams.
   • People didn't like them.

b • No! Travel is easier than before – but there are many traffic jams on the new roads.
   • People don't want to pay.

c • More people have cars today.
   • There are more problems with traffic in cities.

d • Make new roads for cars.
   • People have to pay to use the new roads.

## UNIT 5: SPORTS, WATCH AND LISTEN, EXERCISE 3

| people (e.g. *an old woman*) | a free diver[1] | a young man |
| | old men | scuba divers |
| places (e.g. *a school*) | the sea | Sicily |
| | the world | a city |
| | Italy | a town |
| times of day (e.g. *afternoon*) | evening | morning |
| things (e.g. *a car*) | boats[2] | sand |
| | a scooter[3] | a red balloon[4] |
| | rocks | |

## UNIT 5: SPORT, LISTENING 1, EXERCISE 9

a  They learn quicker and they are faster.
b  tae kwon do
c  They have stronger backs.
d  They think men are bigger, stronger, tougher and faster than women.
e  Are men better than women in all sports?
f  sports science

## UNIT 9, ANIMALS, SPEAKING, EXERCISE 1

### Group C
### Koalas

Koalas live in forests in Australia. Koalas in the north of Australia are smaller than koalas in the south.

Koalas have grey and white fur. Their fur is waterproof. Female koalas have a pocket on the front of their bodies. This pocket, which is called a pouch, is for baby koalas. The name for a baby koala is a joey. The joey lives in the pouch for seven months.

Koalas sleep a lot. Some koalas sleep 18 hours every day. They eat leaves from trees.

# GLOSSARY

| Vocabulary | Pronunciation | Part of speech | Definition |
| --- | --- | --- | --- |
| **UNIT 1** | | | |
| artist | /ˈɑːtɪst/ | (n) | someone who paints, draws or makes sculptures |
| basketball player | /ˈbɑːskɪtbɔːl pleɪə/ | (n) | someone who takes part in a game of basketball |
| brother | /ˈbrʌðə/ | (n) | a man or boy with the same parents as another person |
| businessman | /ˈbɪznɪsmən/ | (n) | a man who works in business, especially if he has a high position in a company |
| businesswoman | /ˈbɪznɪswʊmən/ | (n) | a woman who works in business, especially if she has a high position in a company |
| city | /ˈsɪti/ | (n) | a large town |
| country | /ˈkʌntri/ | (n) | an area of land that has its own government, army, etc. |
| dancer | /ˈdɑːnsə/ | (n) | someone who dances either as a job or for pleasure |
| doctor | /ˈdɒktə/ | (n) | a person whose job is to treat people who are ill or hurt |
| family | /ˈfæməli/ | (n) | a group of people who are related to each other, such as a mother, a father and their children |
| famous | /ˈfeɪməs/ | (adj) | known and recognised by many people |
| fashion designer | /ˈfæʃən dɪˈzaɪnə/ | (n) | a person who creates and plans new clothes |
| father | /ˈfɑːðə/ | (n) | your male parent |
| job | /dʒɒb/ | (n) | the regular work that you do in order to earn money |
| journalist | /ˈdʒɜːnəlɪst/ | (n) | a person who writes news stories or articles for a newspaper or magazine or broadcasts them on radio or television |
| mother | /ˈmʌðə/ | (n) | a female parent |
| name | /neɪm/ | (n) | the word or words that a person, thing or place is known by |
| scientist | /ˈsaɪəntɪst/ | (n) | someone who studies science or works in science |
| singer | /ˈsɪŋə/ | (n) | a person who sings, especially as a job |
| sister | /ˈsɪstə/ | (n) | a girl or woman who has the same parents as another person |
| sportswoman | /ˈspɔːtswʊmən/ | (n) | a woman who plays sport, especially one who plays it well |
| teacher | /ˈtiːtʃə/ | (n) | someone whose job is to teach in a school or college |
| writer | /ˈraɪtə/ | (n) | a person who writes books or articles to be published |
| **UNIT 2** | | | |
| beautiful | /ˈbjuːtɪfəl/ | (adj) | very attractive |
| blue | /bluː/ | (adj) | being the same colour as the sky when there are no clouds |
| cloud | /klaʊd/ | (n) | a white or grey mass in the sky, made of very small drops of water |
| cold | /kəʊld/ | (adj) | having a low temperature |
| desert | /ˈdezət/ | (n) | a large, hot, dry area of land with very few plants |
| forest | /ˈfɒrɪst/ | (n) | a large area of trees growing closely together |
| happy | /ˈhæpi/ | (adj) | feeling, showing or causing pleasure |
| hot | /hɒt/ | (adj) | having a high temperature |
| inside | /ɪnˈsaɪd/ | (prep) | in or into a room, building, container, etc. |
| interesting | /ˈɪntrəstɪŋ/ | (adj) | Someone or something that is interesting keeps your attention because they are unusual, exciting or have a lot of ideas. |
| island | /ˈaɪlənd/ | (n) | a piece of land completely surrounded by water |

| Vocabulary | Pronunciation | Part of speech | Definition |
|---|---|---|---|
| man-made | /mæn'meɪd/ | (adj) | not natural, but made by people |
| natural | /'nætʃərəl/ | (adj) | Something that is natural exists or happens because of nature, not because it was made or done by people. |
| outside | /aʊt'saɪd/ | (adv) | not inside a building |
| path | /pɑːθ/ | (n) | a long, narrow track between one place and another |
| sand | /sænd/ | (n) | a substance that is found on beaches and in deserts, which is made from very small grains of rock |
| sea | /siː/ | (n) | a large area of salt water |
| see | /siː/ | (v) | to notice people and things with your eyes |
| sky | /skaɪ/ | (n) | the area above the Earth, in which clouds, the sun, etc. can be seen |
| snow | /snəʊ/ | (n) | soft white pieces of frozen water that fall from the sky when the weather is cold |
| summer | /'sʌmə/ | (n) | the season of the year between spring and autumn, when the weather is warmest |
| town | /taʊn/ | (n) | a place where people live and work, usually larger than a village but smaller than a city |
| tree | /triː/ | (n) | a tall plant with a thick stem which has branches coming from it and leaves |
| ugly | /'ʌgli/ | (adj) | unpleasant to look at |
| unusual | /ʌn'juːʒəl/ | (adj) | different and not ordinary, often in a way that is interesting or exciting |
| wind | /wɪnd/ | (n) | a natural, fast movement of air |
| winter | /'wɪntə/ | (n) | the coldest season of the year, between autumn and spring |

UNIT 3

| Vocabulary | Pronunciation | Part of speech | Definition |
|---|---|---|---|
| app | /æp/ | (n) | a computer program or piece of software that is designed for a particular purpose that you can download onto a mobile phone or other mobile device |
| biscuit | /'bɪskɪt/ | (n) | a small, flat cake that is dry and usually sweet |
| blog | /blɒg/ | (n) | a record of your activities or opinions that you put on the Internet for other people to read and that you change regularly |
| busy | /'bɪzi/ | (adj) | If you are busy, you are working hard or giving your attention to a particular thing. |
| chat | /tʃæt/ | (v) | to talk to someone in a friendly and informal way |
| chocolate | /'tʃɒklət/ | (n) | a sweet, usually brown, food that is prepared and sold in a block, or a small sweet made from this |
| down | /daʊn/ | (prep) | in or towards a low or lower position, from a higher one |
| download | /daʊn'ləʊd/ | (v) | to copy computer programs, music or other information electronically, especially from the internet or a larger computer |
| eat | /iːt/ | (v) | to put food into your mouth and then swallow it |
| exercise | /'eksəsaɪz/ | (n) | physical activity that you do to make your body strong and healthy |
| follow | /'fɒləʊ/ | (v) | to move behind someone or something and go where they go |
| go out | /gəʊ aʊt/ | (v) | to leave a place in order to go somewhere else |
| gym | /dʒɪm/ | (n) | a building or room with equipment for doing exercises |
| healthy | /'helθi/ | (adj) | good for your health |
| important | /ɪm'pɔːtənt/ | (adj) | valuable, useful or necessary |

| Vocabulary | Pronunciation | Part of speech | Definition |
|---|---|---|---|
| internet | /ˈɪntənet/ | (n) | the system that connects computers all over the world and allows people who use computers to look at websites |
| intonation | /ɪntəʊˈneɪʃən/ | (n) | the way your voice goes up and down when you speak |
| laptop | /ˈlæptɒp/ | (n) | a computer that is small enough to be carried around and used where you are sitting |
| lifestyle | /ˈlaɪfstaɪl/ | (n) | someone's way of living; the things that a person or particular group of people usually do |
| online | /ɒnˈlaɪn/ | (adj) | describes products, services or information that can be bought or used on the Internet |
| polite | /pəˈlaɪt/ | (adj) | behaving in a way that is not rude and shows that you do not only think about yourself |
| post | /pəʊst/ | (v) | to leave a message on a website |
| practise | /ˈpræktɪs/ | (v) | to do or play something regularly or repeatedly in order to become skilled at it |
| record | /rɪˈkɔːd/ | (v) | to store sounds or pictures using electronic equipment, a camera, etc. so that you can listen to them or see them again |
| send | /send/ | (v) | to arrange for something to go or be taken somewhere, especially by post |
| smoke | /sməʊk/ | (v) | to breathe smoke into your mouth from a cigarette |
| survey | /ˈsɜːveɪ/ | (n) | an examination of opinions, behaviour, etc., made by asking people questions |
| up | /ʌp/ | (prep) | vertical or as straight as possible |
| use | /juːz/ | (v) | If you use something, you do something with it for a particular purpose. |
| write | /raɪt/ | (v) | to produce letters, words or numbers on a surface or computer |

UNIT 4

| Vocabulary | Pronunciation | Part of speech | Definition |
|---|---|---|---|
| across | /əˈkrɒs/ | (prep) | on the opposite side of |
| airport | /ˈeəpɔːt/ | (n) | a place where aircraft regularly take off and land, with buildings for passengers to wait in |
| along | /əˈlɒŋ/ | (prep) | from one part of a road, river, etc. to another |
| around | /əˈraʊnd/ | (prep) | to surround or be on all sides of something, or in a circular movement |
| at | /ət/ | (prep) | used to show the place or position of something |
| bank | /bæŋk/ | (n) | an organisation or place where you can borrow money, save money, etc. |
| behind | /bɪˈhaɪnd/ | (prep) | at or to the back of someone or something |
| between | /bɪˈtwiːn/ | (prep) | in the space that separates two places, people or objects |
| bridge | /brɪdʒ/ | (n) | a structure that is built over a river, road, railway, etc. to allow people and vehicles to cross from one side to the other |
| bus station | /ˈbʌs steɪʃən/ | (n) | a building where a bus starts or ends its journey |
| climate | /ˈklaɪmət/ | (n) | the weather conditions that an area usually has |
| clock | /klɒk/ | (n) | a piece of equipment that shows you what time it is, usually in a house or on a building and not worn by a person |
| east | /iːst/ | (n) | the direction that you face to see the sun rise, opposite to the west |
| garden | /ˈgɑːdən/ | (n) | a piece of land belonging to a house, where flowers and other plants are grown |

| Vocabulary | Pronunciation | Part of speech | Definition |
|---|---|---|---|
| here | /hɪə/ | (adv) | in the place where you are |
| hospital | /ˈhɒspɪtəl/ | (n) | a place where ill or injured people go to be treated by doctors and nurses |
| hotel | /həʊˈtel/ | (n) | a place where you pay to stay when you are away from home |
| in | /ɪn/ | (prep) | inside or towards the inside of a container, place or area |
| in front of | /ɪn ˈfrʌnt ɒv/ | (ph) | close to the front part of something |
| into | /ˈɪntə/ | (prep) | towards the inside or middle of something |
| left | /left/ | (adj) | on or towards the side of your body that is to the west when you are facing north |
| library | /ˈlaɪbrəri/ | (n) | a room or building that contains a collection of books and other written material that you can read or borrow |
| modern | /ˈmɒdən/ | (adj) | using the newest ideas, design, technology, etc. and not traditional |
| mosque | /mɒsk/ | (n) | a building for Islamic religious activities and worship |
| new | /njuː/ | (adj) | recently made or having started to exist recently |
| next to | /ˈnekst tuː/ | (ph) | used when describing two people or things that are very close to each other with nothing between them |
| north | /nɔːθ/ | (n) | the direction that is on your left when you face towards the rising sun |
| old | /əʊld/ | (adj) | having lived or existed for many years |
| on | /ɒn/ | (prep) | used to refer to a place when giving directions |
| opposite | /ˈɒpəzɪt/ | (prep) | in a position facing someone or something but on the other side |
| out of | /ˈaʊt ɒv/ | (prep) | used to show movement away from the inside of a place or container |
| over | /ˈəʊvə/ | (prep) | across from one side of something to the other, especially by going up and then down |
| park | /pɑːk/ | (n) | a large area of grass and trees in a city or town, where people can walk and enjoy themselves |
| political | /pəˈlɪtɪkəl/ | (adj) | relating to politics |
| population | /pɒpjəˈleɪʃən/ | (n) | the number of people living in a particular area |
| port | /pɔːt/ | (n) | a town by the sea or by a river which has a harbour, or the harbour itself |
| restaurant | /ˈrestrɒnt/ | (n) | a place where you can buy and eat a meal |
| right | /raɪt/ | (adj) | on or towards the side of your body that is to the east when you are facing north |
| road | /rəʊd/ | (n) | a long, hard surface built for vehicles to drive on |
| satellite | /ˈsætəlaɪt/ | (n) | a device sent up into space to travel round the Earth, used for collecting information or communicating by radio, television, etc. |
| school | /skuːl/ | (n) | a place where children go to be educated |
| south | /saʊθ/ | (n) | the direction which goes towards the part of the Earth below the equator, opposite to the north, or the part of an area or country which is in this direction |
| station | /ˈsteɪʃən/ | (n) | a building where trains stop so that you can get on or off them |
| street | /striːt/ | (n) | a road in a town or city that has houses or other buildings |
| supermarket | /ˈsuːpəmɑːkɪt/ | (n) | a large shop that sells food, drink, products for the home, etc. |
| that | /ðæt/ | (det, pron) | used to refer to something that can be seen or pointed to |

| Vocabulary | Pronunciation | Part of speech | Definition |
|---|---|---|---|
| there | /ðeə/ | (adv) | used when you are pointing or looking at something in order to make someone look in the same direction |
| these | /ðiːz/ | (det, pron) | plural of *this* |
| this | /ðɪs/ | (det, pron) | used to refer to something or someone that can be seen or pointed to |
| those | /ðəʊz/ | (det, pron) | plural of *that* |
| through | /θruː/ | (prep) | from one end or side of something to the other |
| turn | /tɜːn/ | (v) | to change the direction in which you are facing or moving |
| under | /ˈʌndə/ | (prep) | below something, or below the surface of something |
| west | /west/ | (n) | the direction that you face to see the sun go down |

### UNIT 5

| Vocabulary | Pronunciation | Part of speech | Definition |
|---|---|---|---|
| alone | /əˈləʊn/ | (adj) | without other people |
| ancient | /ˈeɪnʃənt/ | (adj) | from a long time ago |
| back | /bæk/ | (n) | the part of your body from your shoulders to your bottom |
| badminton | /ˈbædmɪntən/ | (n) | a sport for two or four people in which you hit a light object with feathers over a net |
| baseball | /ˈbeɪsbɔːl/ | (n) | (the ball used in) a game played by two teams of nine players, in which a player hits a ball with a bat and tries to run around the four corners of a large square area of the field before the other team returns the ball |
| basketball | /ˈbɑːskɪtbɔːl/ | (n) | a game in which two teams try to score points by throwing a ball through a high net, or the ball used in this game |
| bone | /bəʊn/ | (n) | one of the hard pieces that make the structure inside a human or animal |
| competition | /kɒmpəˈtɪʃən/ | (n) | an organised event in which people try to win a prize by being the best, fastest, etc. |
| court | /kɔːt/ | (n) | an area drawn out on the ground that is used for playing sport |
| cycling | /ˈsaɪklɪŋ/ | (n) | the sport or activity of riding a bicycle |
| fan | /fæn/ | (n) | someone who admires and supports a person, sport, sports team, etc. |
| fast | /fɑːst/ | (adj) | moving or happening quickly, or able to move or happen quickly |
| fat | /fæt/ | (adj) | Someone who is fat weighs too much. |
| fit | /fɪt/ | (adj) | healthy and strong, especially as a result of exercise |
| football | /ˈfʊtbɔːl/ | (n) | a game in which two teams of players kick a round ball and try to score goals |
| goal | /gəʊl/ | (n) | a point scored in sports such as football, when a player sends a ball or other object into a particular area, such as between two posts |
| good | /gʊd/ | (adj) | of a high quality or level |
| hard | /hɑːd/ | (adj) | difficult to understand or do |
| horse riding | /ˈhɔːs raɪdɪŋ/ | (n) | the sport or activity of riding a horse |
| Japanese | /dʒæpənˈiːz/ | (adj) | coming from or relating to Japan |
| judo | /ˈdʒuːdəʊ/ | (n) | a sport from Japan in which two people try to throw each other to the ground |
| karate | /kəˈrɑːti/ | (n) | a sport from Japan in which people fight with the hands or feet |

| Vocabulary | Pronunciation | Part of speech | Definition |
|---|---|---|---|
| kung fu | /kʌŋˈfuː/ | (n) | a sport from China in which people fight using their hands and feet |
| loser | /ˈluːzə/ | (n) | someone who does not win a game or competition |
| million | /ˈmɪljən/ | (n) | the number 1,000,000 |
| pilates | /pɪˈlɑːtiːz/ | (n) | a system of physical exercise involving controlled movements, stretching and breathing |
| player | /ˈpleɪə/ | (n) | someone who takes part in a game or sport |
| point | /pɔɪnt/ | (n) | a unit used for showing who is winning in a game or competition |
| popular | /ˈpɒpjələ/ | (adj) | liked by many people |
| professional | /prəˈfeʃənəl/ | (adj) | Someone is professional if they earn money for a sport or activity which most people do as a hobby. |
| quick | /kwɪk/ | (adj) | doing something fast |
| rugby | /ˈrʌgbi/ | (n) | a sport played by two teams with an oval ball and H-shaped goals |
| running | /ˈrʌnɪŋ/ | (n) | the sport of moving on your feet at a speed faster than walking |
| score | /skɔː/ | (n) | the number of points someone gets in a game or test |
| skiing | /ˈskiːɪŋ/ | (n) | the sport of moving over snow on skis |
| slow | /sləʊ/ | (adj) | doing, moving or happening without much speed |
| strong | /strɒŋ/ | (adj) | physically powerful |
| swimming | /swɪmɪŋ/ | (n) | the activity of moving through water by moving your body |
| tall | /tɔːl/ | (adj) | having a greater than average height |
| team | /tiːm/ | (n) | a group of people who play a sport or game together against another group of players |
| tennis | /ˈtenɪs/ | (n) | a sport in which two or four people hit a small ball to each other over a net |
| thin | /θɪn/ | (adj) | Something that is thin is smaller than usual between its opposite sides. |
| traditional | /trəˈdɪʃənəl/ | (adj) | following the customs or ways of behaving that have continued in a group of people or society for a long time |
| unfit | /ʌnˈfɪt/ | (adj) | not healthy because you do too little exercise |
| unhappy | /ʌnˈhæpi/ | (adj) | sad |
| unhealthy | /ʌnˈhelθi/ | (adj) | likely to become ill or likely to damage your health |
| volleyball | /ˈvɒlibɔːl/ | (n) | a game in which two teams use their hands to hit a ball over a net without allowing it to touch the ground |
| weak | /wiːk/ | (adj) | not physically strong |
| winner | /ˈwɪnə/ | (n) | someone who wins a game or competition |
| yoga | /ˈjəʊgə/ | (n) | a set of exercises for the mind and body |
| UNIT 6 | | | |
| accountant | /əˈkaʊntənt/ | (n) | someone whose job is to keep or examine the financial records of a person or organisation |
| architect | /ˈɑːkɪtekt/ | (n) | someone whose job is to design buildings |
| banker | /ˈbæŋkə/ | (n) | someone with an important position within a bank |
| boring | /ˈbɔːrɪŋ/ | (adj) | not interesting or exciting |
| builder | /ˈbɪldə/ | (n) | a person whose job it is to make buildings |
| clever | /ˈklevə/ | (adj) | able to learn and understand things quickly and easily |
| engineer | /endʒɪˈnɪə/ | (n) | someone whose job is to design, build or repair machines, engines, roads, bridges, etc. |

| Vocabulary | Pronunciation | Part of speech | Definition |
|---|---|---|---|
| experience | /ɪkˈspɪəriəns/ | (n) | knowledge that you get from doing a job, or from doing, seeing or feeling something |
| farmer | /ˈfɑːmə/ | (n) | someone who owns or looks after a farm |
| fire | /faɪə/ | (n) | heat, light and flames that are produced when something burns |
| fireman | /ˈfaɪəmən/ | (n) | a man whose job is to stop fires burning |
| friendly | /ˈfrendli/ | (adj) | behaving in a pleasant, kind way towards someone |
| good-looking | /gʊdˈlʊkɪŋ/ | (adj) | If someone is good-looking, they have an attractive face. |
| helpful | /ˈhelpfəl/ | (adj) | willing to help, or useful |
| kind | /kaɪnd/ | (adj) | generous, helpful and thinking about other people's feelings |
| lawyer | /ˈlɔɪə/ | (n) | someone whose job is to give advice to people about the law and speak for them in court |
| musician | /mjuːˈzɪʃən/ | (n) | someone who plays a musical instrument, often as a job |
| nurse | /nɜːs/ | (n) | someone whose job is to care for ill and injured people |
| opinion | /əˈpɪnjən/ | (n) | a thought or belief about something or someone |
| pilot | /ˈpaɪlət/ | (n) | someone who flies an aircraft |
| policeman | /pəˈliːsmən/ | (n) | a man who is a member of the police |
| reason | /ˈriːzən/ | (n) | the facts about why something happens or why someone does something |
| slim | /slɪm/ | (adj) | Someone who is slim is thin in an attractive way. |
| take off | /teɪk ˈɑf/ | (v) | If an aircraft, bird or insect takes off, it leaves the ground and begins to fly. |
| time | /taɪm/ | (n) | a particular point in the day or night |
| waiter | /ˈweɪtə/ | (n) | a man who works in a restaurant, bringing food to customers |

UNIT 7

| Vocabulary | Pronunciation | Part of speech | Definition |
|---|---|---|---|
| agree | /əˈgriː/ | (v) | to have the same opinion as someone |
| apartment | /əˈpɑːtmənt/ | (n) | a set of rooms for living in, especially on one floor of a building |
| change | /tʃeɪndʒ/ | (v) | to stop having or using one thing, and start having or using another |
| cheap | /tʃiːp/ | (adj) | costing little money or less than is usual or expected |
| clean | /kliːn/ | (adj) | not dirty |
| collect | /kəˈlekt/ | (v) | to go to a place and bring someone or something away from it |
| comfortable | /ˈkʌmftəbəl/ | (adj) | describes furniture, clothes, etc. that provide a pleasant feeling and that do not give you any pain |
| day trip | /ˈdeɪ trɪp/ | (n) | a visit to a place in which you go there and come back on the same day |
| different | /ˈdɪfərənt/ | (adj) | not the same |
| dirty | /ˈdɜːti/ | (adj) | not clean |
| disagree | /dɪsəˈgriː/ | (v) | to have a different opinion from someone else about something |
| expensive | /ɪkˈspensɪv/ | (adj) | costing a lot of money |
| far (away) | /fɑː (əˈweɪ)/ | (adv) | at, to or from a great distance in space or time |
| fresh | /freʃ/ | (adj) | Fresh food has been produced or collected recently and has not been frozen, dried, etc. |
| glass | /glɑːs/ | (n) | a hard, transparent substance that objects such as windows and bottles are made of |
| hungry | /ˈhʌngri/ | (adj) | wanting or needing food |

| Vocabulary | Pronunciation | Part of speech | Definition |
|---|---|---|---|
| leather | /ˈleðə/ | (n) | the skin of animals that is used to make things such as shoes and bags |
| manage | /ˈmænɪdʒ/ | (v) | to be in control of an office, shop, team, etc. |
| manager | /ˈmænɪdʒə/ | (n) | someone in control of an office, shop, team, etc. |
| metal | /ˈmetəl/ | (n) | a usually hard, shiny material such as iron, gold or silver which heat and electricity can travel through |
| narrow | /ˈnærəʊ/ | (adj) | Narrow things measure a small distance from one side to the other. |
| near | /nɪə/ | (adj) | close in distance |
| noisy | /ˈnɔɪzi/ | (adj) | making a lot of noise |
| normal | /ˈnɔːməl/ | (adj) | usual, ordinary and expected |
| paint | /peɪnt/ | (n) | a coloured liquid that you put on a surface such as a wall to decorate it, or that you use to produce a picture |
| pay | /peɪ/ | (v) | to give money to someone because you are buying something from them, or because you owe them money |
| plastic | /ˈplæstɪk/ | (adj) | made of plastic |
| psychologist | /saɪˈkɒlədʒɪst/ | (n) | someone who studies the human mind and human emotions and behaviour, and how different situations have an effect on them |
| quiet | /ˈkwaɪət/ | (adj) | making little or no noise |
| quite | /kwaɪt/ | (adv) | a little or a lot but not completely |
| roof | /ruːf/ | (n) | the surface that covers the top of a building or vehicle |
| sad | /sæd/ | (adj) | unhappy or making you feel unhappy |
| same | /seɪm/ | (adj) | not another different person, thing or situation |
| thirsty | /ˈθɜːsti/ | (adj) | needing to drink |
| traditional | /trəˈdɪʃənəl/ | (adj) | following the customs or ways of behaving that have continued in a group of people or society for a long time |
| way | /weɪ/ | (n) | the route you take to get from one place to another |
| wooden | /ˈwʊdən/ | (adj) | made of wood |

## UNIT 8

| Vocabulary | Pronunciation | Part of speech | Definition |
|---|---|---|---|
| apple | /ˈæpəl/ | (n) | a hard, round fruit that has a green or red skin and is white inside |
| banana | /bəˈnɑːnə/ | (n) | a long, curved fruit with a yellow skin |
| bean | /biːn/ | (n) | a seed, or the pod containing seeds, of various climbing plants, eaten as a vegetable |
| beef | /biːf/ | (n) | the meat of a cow |
| bread | /bred/ | (n) | a basic food made by mixing flour, water and sometimes yeast |
| cheese | /tʃiːz/ | (n) | a food made from milk, which can either be firm or soft and is usually yellow or white in colour |
| chicken | /ˈtʃɪkɪn/ | (n) | a type of bird kept on a farm for its eggs or its meat |
| fact | /fækt/ | (n) | something that you know is true, exists or has happened |
| fast food | /fɑstˈfuːd/ | (n) | hot food that can be served very quickly because it is already prepared |
| feed | /fiːd/ | (v) | to give food to a person, group or animal |
| festival | /ˈfestəvəl/ | (n) | a special day or period when people celebrate something, especially a religious event |
| first | /fɜːrst/ | (adv) | before everything or everyone else |

| Vocabulary | Pronunciation | Part of speech | Definition |
|---|---|---|---|
| fish | /fɪʃ/ | (n) | an animal that lives only in water and swims using its tail and fins |
| fruit | /fruːt/ | (n) | something such as an apple or orange that grows on a tree or a bush, contains seeds and can be eaten as food |
| grow | /grəʊ/ | (v) | If a plant grows, or you grow it, it develops from a seed to a full plant. |
| half | /hɑːf/ | (n) | one of two equal parts of something |
| holiday | /ˈhɒlədeɪ/ | (n) | a time when you do not have to go to work or school |
| international | /ɪntəˈnæʃənəl/ | (adj) | relating to or involving two or more countries |
| lamb | /læm/ | (n) | a young sheep, or the flesh of a young sheep eaten as meat |
| last | /lɑːst/ | (adv) | used to talk about the most recent time you did something |
| lemon | /ˈlemən/ | (n) | an oval, yellow fruit that has sour juice |
| meat | /miːt/ | (n) | muscles and other soft parts of animals, used as food |
| milk | /mɪlk/ | (n) | a white liquid produced by women and other female animals, such as cows |
| noodles | /ˈnuːdəlz/ | (n) | thin pieces of pasta (= food made from flour and water) |
| orange | /ˈɒrɪndʒ/ | (n) | a round, sweet fruit that has a thick, orange skin and an orange centre divided into many parts |
| pepper | /ˈpepə/ | (n) | a hollow green, red or yellow vegetable |
| pie chart | /ˈpaɪ tʃɑːt/ | (n) | a circle which is divided from its centre into several parts to show how a total amount is divided up |
| poor | /pɔːr/ | (adj) | having very little money or few possessions |
| rice | /raɪs/ | (n) | small grains from a plant that are cooked and eaten |
| rich | /rɪtʃ/ | (adj) | having much more money than most people, or owning things that could be sold for a lot of money |
| second | /ˈsekənd/ | (adv) | after one other person or thing in order or importance |
| special | /ˈspeʃəl/ | (adj) | better or more important than usual things |
| spend | /spend/ | (v) | to use money to buy or pay for something |
| sweet | /swiːt/ | (n) | a small piece of sweet food, often made of sugar or chocolate |
| third | /θɜːrd/ | (adv) | '3rd' written as a word |
| vegetable | /ˈvedʒtəbəl/ | (n) | a plant that you eat, for example potatoes, onions, beans, etc. |

### UNIT 9

| Vocabulary | Pronunciation | Part of speech | Definition |
|---|---|---|---|
| angry | /ˈæŋgri/ | (adj) | having a strong feeling against someone who has behaved badly, making you want to shout at them or hurt them |
| beak | /biːk/ | (n) | the hard, pointed part of a bird's mouth |
| brain | /breɪn/ | (n) | the organ inside your head that controls thought, memory, feelings and activity |
| camel | /ˈkæməl/ | (n) | a large animal that lives in the desert and has one or two raised parts on its back |
| climb | /klaɪm/ | (v) | to use your legs, or your legs and hands, to go up or onto the top of something |
| cup | /kʌp/ | (n) | a small, round container, often with a handle, used for drinking tea, coffee, etc. |
| cut | /kʌt/ | (v) | to use a knife or other sharp tool to divide something, remove part of something, or make a hole in something |
| grass | /grɑːs/ | (n) | a common plant with narrow green leaves that grows close to the ground |

| Vocabulary | Pronunciation | Part of speech | Definition |
|---|---|---|---|
| hand | /hænd/ | (n) | the part of your body on the end of your arm that has fingers and a thumb |
| jump | /dʒʌmp/ | (v) | to push your body up and away from the ground using your feet and legs |
| jungle | /ˈdʒʌŋgəl/ | (n) | a tropical forest in which trees and plants grow very closely together |
| kangaroo | /kæŋgərˈuː/ | (n) | a large Australian animal that moves by jumping on its back legs |
| long | /lɒŋ/ | (adj) | having a large distance from one end to the other |
| nest | /nest/ | (n) | a structure built by birds or insects to leave their eggs in to develop |
| orangutan | /ɔːˈræŋuːtæn/ | (n) | a large ape with reddish-brown hair and long arms which lives in the forests of Sumatra and Borneo |
| rabbit | /ˈræbɪt/ | (n) | a small animal with fur and long ears that lives in a hole in the ground |
| race | /reɪs/ | (n) | a competition in which people run, ride, drive, etc. against each other in order to see who is the fastest |
| road sign | /ˈrəʊd saɪn/ | (n) | a notice on a road giving information, directions, a warning, etc. |
| sharp | /ʃɑːp/ | (adj) | having a very thin or pointed edge that can cut things |
| stick | /stɪk/ | (n) | a long, thin piece of wood, usually broken or fallen from a tree |
| tired | /taɪəd/ | (adj) | feeling that you want to rest or sleep |
| wet | /wet/ | (adj) | covered in water or another liquid |
| wild | /waɪld/ | (adj) | A wild animal or plant lives or grows in its natural environment and not where people live. |

UNIT 10

| Vocabulary | Pronunciation | Part of speech | Definition |
|---|---|---|---|
| accident | /ˈæksɪdənt/ | (n) | something bad which happens that is not expected or intended, and which causes injury or damage |
| air-conditioned | /ˈeəkəndɪʃənd/ | (adj) | having air conditioning |
| arrive | /əˈraɪv/ | (v) | to reach a place, especially at the end of a journey |
| bicycle | /ˈbaɪsɪkəl/ | (n) | a two-wheeled vehicle that you sit on and move by turning the two pedals |
| board | /bɔːd/ | (v) | to get onto or allow people to get onto a boat, train or aircraft |
| boat | /bəʊt/ | (n) | a vehicle for travelling on water |
| break | /breɪk/ | (v) | to separate into two or more pieces or to make something do this |
| bus | /bʌs/ | (n) | a large vehicle in which people are driven from one place to another |
| car | /kɑː/ | (n) | a road vehicle with an engine, four wheels and seats for a small number of people |
| check in | /ˈtʃek ɪn/ | (v) | to go to the desk at an airport, so that you can be told where you will be sitting and so that your bags can be put on the aircraft |
| commuter | /kəˈmjuːtə/ | (n) | someone who regularly travels between work and home |
| congestion | /kənˈdʒestʃən/ | (n) | when there is too much traffic and movement is made difficult |
| depart | /dɪˈpɑːt/ | (v) | to go away or leave, especially on a journey |
| destination | /destɪˈneɪʃən/ | (n) | the place where someone or something is going |
| ferry | /ˈferi/ | (n) | a boat that regularly carries passengers and often vehicles across an area of water |
| flight | /flaɪt/ | (n) | a journey through air or space in an aircraft or other vehicle |
| fly | /flaɪ/ | (v) | to travel through the air in an aircraft |
| frozen | /ˈfrəʊzən/ | (adj) | turned into ice |

| Vocabulary | Pronunciation | Part of speech | Definition |
|---|---|---|---|
| get stuck | /get ˈstʌk/ | (v) | to become unable to move, or fixed in a particular position |
| goods | /gʊdz/ | (n) | items which are made to be sold |
| hole | /həʊl/ | (n) | a hollow space in something, or an opening in a surface |
| ice | /aɪs/ | (n) | water that has frozen and become solid |
| introduce | /ˌɪntrəˈdʒuːs/ | (v) | to tell someone another person's name the first time that they meet |
| journey | /ˈdʒɜːni/ | (n) | when you travel from one place to another |
| land | /lænd/ | (v) | to arrive at a place in a plane or a boat, or to make a plane or a boat reach the land |
| metro railway | /ˈmetrəʊ ˈreɪlweɪ/ | (n) | an electric railway system in some cities |
| motorbike | /ˈməʊtəbaɪk/ | (n) | a vehicle with two wheels and an engine |
| need | /niːd/ | (v) | If you need something, you must have it. |
| passenger | /ˈpæsəndʒə/ | (n) | someone who is travelling in a vehicle but is not controlling it |
| petrol | /ˈpetrəl/ | (n) | a liquid fuel used in cars |
| plane | /pleɪn/ | (n) | a vehicle that flies and has at least one engine and wings |
| private | /ˈpraɪvɪt/ | (adj) | only for one person or group and not for everyone |
| public | /ˈpʌblɪk/ | (adj) | provided by the government from taxes to be available to everyone |
| reserve | /rɪˈzɜːv/ | (v) | to arrange to have a seat on an aircraft, a room in a hotel, etc. |
| ride | /raɪd/ | (v) | to travel by sitting on a horse, bicycle or motorcycle and controlling it |
| river taxi | /ˈrɪvə ˈtæksi/ | (n) | a small boat on a river, operated by a person who you pay to take you where you want to go |
| road rage | /ˈrəʊd reɪdʒ/ | (n) | anger and violence between drivers |
| sky train | /ˈskaɪ treɪn/ | (n) | a railway system that has a single rail above ground level, or the train that travels along it |
| solution | /səˈluːʃən/ | (n) | the answer to a problem |
| stand | /stænd/ | (v) | to be in a vertical position on your feet |
| taxi | /ˈtæksi/ | (n) | a car with a driver who you pay to take you somewhere |
| ticket | /ˈtɪkɪt/ | (n) | a small piece of paper that shows you have paid to do something, for example travel on a bus, watch a film, etc. |
| traffic | /ˈtræfɪk/ | (n) | the cars, trucks, etc. using a road |
| traffic jam | /ˈtræfɪk dʒæm/ | (n) | a line of cars, trucks, etc. that are moving slowly or not moving at all |
| train | /treɪn/ | (n) | a long, thin vehicle which travels along metal tracks and carries people or goods |
| tram | /træm/ | (n) | an electric vehicle for carrying passengers, mostly in cities, which moves along metal lines in the road |
| transport system | /ˈtrænspɔːt ˈsɪstəm/ | (n) | a system of vehicles, such as buses, trains, aircraft, etc., for getting from one place to another |
| travelator | /ˈtrævəleɪtə/ | (n) | a moving pavement for transporting pedestrians, such as in an airport |
| the underground | /ˈʌndəgraʊnd/ | (ph) | a system of trains that is built under a town or city |
| useless | /ˈjuːsləs/ | (adj) | If something is useless, it does not work well or it has no effect. |

# VIDEO AND AUDIO SCRIPTS

## UNIT 1

### ▶ The film makers

This is a video about people who make nature films. Let's meet them. This is Glenn Evans. Glenn's a cameraman. He makes films all over the world. Every good cameraman needs a good sound man. This is Jonah Torreano. Jonah likes having fun.

And this is Todd Brown. Todd's the assistant, so he helps the team. Jud Cremata's the producer. Jud's job is to plan travel and equipment for the crew.

The crew are in Alaska. They are going to the airport with Jeff Corwin. Jeff is a nature expert. He's also a TV presenter. You can see all their bags here. Film crews have a lot of equipment. They are going from Palmer to Kaktovik. Kaktovik is a small place. Only 300 people live there. The crew take their camera to the ice. They want to film some polar bears. They make camp. The crew start their search for a polar bear. They go by helicopter. They see a seal – food for polar bears – and tracks from the polar bears in the snow. The film crew know they are near. Jeff gets out of the helicopter to look at the polar bears' tracks on the ground. Finally, they see *three* polar bears! The crew film the family of bears from the safety of their helicopter. The film makers make their film and go home happy.

### 🔊 1.1

1 introduce   2 please   3 Peru   4 Turkey
5 twenty   6 eighteen   7 study   8 business
9 computer   10 producer

### 🔊 1.2

**Carlos:** Hi, hello. I'm Carlos. I'm going to tell you about Koko. She's a student in our class. She's 18 and she's from Japan. Her family's from Sapporo. Her father's a teacher. She wants to study English at university.

**Kerry:** A-l-l right! Thank you, Carlos. So, Koko. It's your turn. Please introduce the student next to you.

**Koko:** Hello! Yes! I'm going to tell you about Hussain. This is Hussain. He's from Al Ain. Al Ain is in, the uh …

**Kerry:** Un-*it*-ed … A-rab … *Em*-ir-ates.

**Koko:** Yes … the UAE! Hussain's from Al Ain. It's in the UAE. He's 20. His family's from Al Ain. He has two younger sisters and one younger brother. He likes football and his favourite footballer is Lionel Messi. Hussain wants to study Business at university.

**Kerry:** Thank you, Koko. Well done. So, Hussain. Please introduce the student next to you.

**Hussain:** Hello! I'm going to tell you about Nehir. Nehir is 19. She's from Turkey. She has a brother. Her family has a hotel. She wants to study Business at university.

**Kerry:** Thank you, Hussain. Nehir – your turn!

**Nehir:** Hello. I'm going to tell you about Carlos. He's 19. He's from Peru. His father's a TV producer and his mother's a doctor. Carlos wants to study Computer Science at university.

**Kerry:** Thank you, Nehir.

### 🔊 1.3

**A**

**Kerry:** That's a lovely photograph, Mehmet.

**Mehmet:** Thank you. It's a photograph of my friend.

**Kerry:** What's her name?

**Mehmet:** Meral.

**Kerry:** Is she from Turkey?

**Mehmet:** Yes, but she isn't from Ankara like me. She's from Izmir.

**B**

**Ryo:** Excuse me, Kerry. Are you from London?

**Kerry:** No, no, I'm not from England. I'm from Australia. But my grandparents are English. They aren't from London. They're from Manchester.

**Ryo:** Are your parents Australian?

**Kerry:** Yes – and my sisters. We're all Australian.

### 🔊 1.4

1 fashion designer   2 sportswoman
3 businesswoman   4 businessman
5 basketball player   6 scientist

### 🔊 1.5

**Marie:** Hi! Good morning, everybody!

**All:** Morning. / Hi. / Hello,

**Marie:** I'm going to tell you about two famous people from the United States. One person is a famous man and one person is a famous woman. So … picture one. Who's this? In the photograph? Do you know?

**Student:** Um, is he an actor?

**Marie:** Uh, no, no, he isn't an actor. Anybody? No? OK, well, this is Larry Page. And he has a famous company: Google. I'm sure you know it! Larry's father's name is Carl and his mother's name is Gloria. They're computer scientists.

And, OK, now this photograph. This is Ursula Burns. She's a famous businesswoman. She's from New York but her family's Latin American. They're from Panama. She's famous for her work with Xerox. She's the first …

**Clare:** … thank you, Marie. Hi! Now I'm going to tell you about two famous people from the United Kingdom. This one, this is Jessica Ennis-Hill. She's a sportswoman and she's from Sheffield, a city in England. Her father's from Jamaica and her mother's from England. Jessica has a lot of medals for athletics.

A-a-and this is my next photograph. This is Sir Harry Kroto. He's a famous scientist from England. He has a Nobel Prize. He's from a small town near Cambridge. His wife's name is Margaret. She's a scientist too.

**1.6**

**1** I'm going to tell you about two famous people from Mexico.

**2** One person is a famous woman and one person is a famous man.

**3** Ana García is a famous Mexican chef.

**4** This is Carlos Slim.

**5** He's a famous Mexican businessman.

 **1.7**

er

sign-er

de–<u>sign</u>-er

mous de-<u>sign</u>-er

<u>fa</u>-mous de-<u>sign</u>-er

a <u>fa</u>-mous de-<u>sign</u>-er

she's a <u>fam</u>-ous de-<u>sign</u>-er

 **1.8**

**1** I'm going to tell you about two famous people from Egypt.

**2** Karim Abdel Aziz is a famous actor.

**3** Carmen Suleiman's a famous singer.

**4** Karim's father is Mohammed Abdel Aziz.

**5** He's a film director.

**6** Karim's aunt is Samira Muhsin.

**7** She's an actor.

# UNIT 2

### Seasons in North America

Around the world, seasons and the weather are different. Why is this? Why are there two seasons in some countries – a dry season and a rainy season – but four seasons in others – summer, autumn, winter and spring? This red line is the equator. Above and below the equator are two zones: the Tropic of Cancer and the Tropic of Capricorn. Countries that are on the equator or in these two zones have hot weather. Parts of Kenya are on the equator. They have two seasons. It is hot all year round, but it rains from April to June and October to December. Egypt is in the Tropic of Cancer. The wet season is from December to April. Above and below the tropics, the weather is different.

In this video, we're going to look at seasons in the United States and Canada. Spring in the United States and Canada is from March to May. The weather is warm and wet. In Alaska, the rainfall is over 400 centimetres a year, but in Arizona, it is only eight centimetres a year. There's a lot of rain and sun. Plants and flowers grow at this time. After spring comes summer. The summer months are June, July and August. It is hot and sunny. There's no school in the summer, so children play outside. You can sometimes see storms in the summer, but usually there are blue skies. In summer, the plants and trees have lots of green leaves, and fruit and vegetables grow. Autumn is between September and November. The weather is

cold and it can be misty in the morning and evening. Many people like the autumn because the leaves on the trees change colour and fall. It can be very beautiful. Winter is from December to February. Winter is cold and there can be a lot of snow. It can be as cold as minus 60 degrees Celsius. You can see snow in the cities and in the country. Snow can be dangerous for cars, but children like it, and many people go skiing. Some people hate the cold weather; they travel south to the tropics for the sun and hot weather. Do you like hot or cold seasons?

 **2.1**

**1** Today, I want to **look** at **some**thing **new**.

**2** **Take** a **look** at this **photograph**.

**3** There's a **beautiful beach** next to a **blue sea**.

**4** It's **win**ter and there's a **moun**tain.

**5** It's **hot** and there's **sand** and there are **rocks**.

 **2.2**

**Professor:** OK, so … Today, I want to look at something new. I want to talk about *man*-made places – *man*-made environments in other words.

Take a look at photograph 1. What can we see? Well, it's a hot day in summer. There's a beautiful beach next to a blue sea. There are people on the beach. But look again. In fact, it's *not* summer – it's winter and there's snow outside. In other words, the beach, the sea – they're not natural. They're *man*-made … but the people are real. This place is the Ocean Dome. It's in Japan.

And here, photograph 2, what can we see? Well, it's winter and there's a mountain. There's a lot of snow and people are skiing. Where is this? Canada? The north-west United States?

Well, in fact, this is, again, a *man*-made environment. The snow's inside, but outside it's a hot summer's day. This is a photograph of the Snow Centre near London.

And now photograph 3. Here, we can see a desert. It's hot and there's sand and there are rocks. Now, where do you think this is? … anybody? Well, this is in Nebraska in the United States. It's cold and there's snow outside. But inside … well, you can see for yourself. A hot desert place.

Now, what can these *man*-made places tell us about Zygmunt Bauman's ideas of …

 **2.3**

**1** There's a lot of rain in the monsoon season in Thailand.

**2** Russia gets a lot of snow in winter.

**3** The dry season in Brazil begins in May.

**4** Spring in England is from March to May.

**5** In autumn, the trees change colour from green to orange or red in Japan.

**6** In Australia, summer begins in December and ends in February.

**7** The rainy season in Nigeria is from March to October.

**2.4**

January, February, March, April, May, June, July, August, September, October, November, December

 **2.5**

**Daniela:** OK, so, good morning, everybody. I'm Daniela. OK, so, uh, I'm going to talk about two photographs of a place in spring. I'm from Naples in Italy and I don't like to talk about cold places or places in winter – no, really, it's true!

OK, so here's my first photograph. This isn't in Italy. It's in Turkey. It's actually an island. And there's a town here. You can see there are a lot of white buildings. It's a beautiful day in spring; very sunny, very nice.

There's a nice forest there and … my next photograph … is from the forest. There's a park and it's good to go there when it's a hot day.

And there's the town … and the sea, which is beautiful and blue.

OK, so I chose these photographs because …

**Altan:** Hello, everybody! OK, so, I'm Altan. I'm from Samsun. Uh, Samsun is in Turkey, I'm Turkish, and Samsun's a city by the Black Sea. But, OK, so today I'm going to talk about a different place.

Here's my first photograph. It's a beautiful place. You can see there's a big mountain and there are trees here. It's sunny, but it's a cold day in autumn. Can you see the colour of the trees? All red and yellow.

So, where is this beautiful place? Well, it's in South Korea. This is Seoraksan National Park. It's a famous park.

Here's another photograph of the park. It's sunny but in fact it's cold. A lot of people go there.

 **2.6**

a OK, so, good morning, everybody. I'm Daniela.
b OK, so, I'm going to talk about two photographs of a place in spring.
c OK, so here's my first photograph.
d Hello, everybody! OK, so, I'm Altan.
e I'm from Samsun. Samsun is in Turkey.
f Here's my first photograph.
g Here's another photograph of the park.

 **2.7**

**Khaled:** Hello everybody! OK, so I'm Khaled. I'm from Port Said. OK, so today I'm going to talk about two photographs of a place in spring. Here's my first photograph. You can see there's a big mountain. There's a lot of snow. And there are trees. The trees are green. OK, so where is this place? It's in Japan. This is Mount Fuji.

Here's another photograph of the mountain. There's a path and you can see there are people there. There are a lot of white clouds below. It's a beautiful place. I want to go there.

 **2.8**

1 There's a park.
2 There's a nice forest.
3 And there are trees here.
4 You can see there's a mountain in the photograph.
5 You can see there are a lot of white buildings.

 **2.9**

1 There's a river in the photograph.
2 There's snow on the mountains.
3 There are people on the beach.
4 There are trees in the garden.
5 There's a small town in the mountains.
6 There's a red car in the desert.
7 There are black clouds in the sky.

# UNIT 3

## ▶ The Bedouin

Sinai in Egypt is a land of mountains and desert. It's difficult to live here, but for thousands of years, people – called the Bedouin – have lived here. For the Bedouin, the desert provides everything they need. They follow their camels through the desert. They only use what their camels can carry. Once, there were around 300,000 Bedouin in the desert, but today there are only 22,000. Doctor Ahmed is the last Bedouin healer in Sinai. He uses plants from the desert to make traditional medicines. He helps people who cannot reach a hospital. Now that Doctor Ahmed is old, he wants to give his knowledge of traditional medicine to a new generation. His six pupils have learnt many things, like making medicine. He takes the boys 160 kilometres into the desert – but they will have to get home on their own. For a journey through the desert, the Bedouin need a camel. Doctor Ahmed shows them how to choose a good one.

Ahmed watches the boys start for home. Doctor Ahmed waits for them at his clinic. The boys arrive back tired, but safe. A very proud moment for their Bedouin teacher.

 **3.1**

**Speaker A:** What's your name?
**Jennifer:** Jennifer.
**Speaker A:** Are you from New York?
**Jennifer:** No. I'm from London.

 **3.2**

1 Can you tell me about the video?
2 What's the problem?
3 That's a good question.
4 Do you need money for the gym?
5 I like to be healthy.
6 The university has a gym.

**3.3**

**A**

**Son:**   ... it's going to be cold this winter. Reeeaally, really cold.

**Father:**   OK, so what's the problem?

**Son:**   Well, you know how I like to be healthy and do exercise ...

**Father:**   Yes, OK ...

**Son:**   The thing is, the university has a gym.

**Father:**   Ah! And the gym is warm?

**Son:**   Yes, it is. It's warm. I usually do exercise in the park, but this winter ...

**Father:**   Do you need money for the gym?

**Son:**   Well, ...

**B**

**Lecturer:**   Um, Yes? Yes, the young man at the back there.

**Student:**   Thank you, Professor Davies, for such an interesting lecture. But I have a question ...

**Lecturer:**   Sure. Please, go ahead.

**Student:**   In the United States, do most young people live on their own now? I mean, do they have their own home? And they don't live with their family?

**Lecturer:**   Ah! That's a good question. Yes, it *is* true, but only in some places. For example, New York and Los Angeles but not ...

**C**

**Student A:**   Here's your coffee.

**Student B:**   Oh thanks!

**Student A:**   I got some chocolate biscuits as well.

**Student B:**   Ooh! Nice!

**Student A:**   So, um, can you tell me about the video? What was it about?

**Student B:**   Hmmm. Sorry! Yeah, it was really, really good.

**Student A:**   Oh?

**Student B:**   Yeah, so, it was about lifestyles of people in Canada. It's very cold there and so ...

 **3.4**

Saturday; Wednesday; Friday; Tuesday; Sunday; Thursday; Monday

 **3.5**

This is Élodie. She's from France. She takes the bus to university every day. The bus comes at seven thirty. Élodie arrives at eight thirty. She has a biology lecture at nine on Tuesday and Thursday. She has lunch with her friends at twelve thirty. Élodie has an English class at three o'clock in the afternoon. She goes to the cinema with her family on Friday evening.

 **3.6**

**1**

**Female speaker 1:**   Excuse me! Can I ask you some questions?

**Female speaker 2:**   I don't have time, I'm sorry.

**2**

**Male speaker 1:**   I'd like to ask some questions – is that OK?

**Male speaker 2:**   Yes, sure.

**3**

**Sultan:**   Good morning! I'm Sultan.

**Jack:**   Nice to meet you! I'm Jack.

**4**

**Female speaker 3:**   Do you drink a lot of coffee?

**Female speaker 4:**   No, not really.

**5**

**Male speaker 3:**   I play football for my country.

**Male speaker 4:**   Really?

**6**

**Female speaker 5:**   I watch a lot of films.

**Female speaker 6:**   I see.

 **3.7**

**April:**   Good morning! Can I ask you ...?

**Woman 1:**   Sorry, sorry, no time! no time!

**April:**   Excuse me! Do you have ...?

**Woman 2:**   Sorry! Can't stop! That's my bus!

**April:**   Excuse me! Can I have a few minutes of your time?

**Jasvinder:**   Uh, yes, sure.

**April:**   Great! My name's April. I'm a student at the university and I'm asking people questions about their lifestyle. I'd like to ask you some questions – is that OK?

**Jasvinder:**   Yes, no problem. I'm Jasvinder.

**April:**   Great! Nice to meet you, Jasvinder! OK, so, uh, well, I'll just start, then? OK, so do you live with your parents?

**Jasvinder:**   Yes.

**April:**   And do you work or study?

**Jasvinder:**   Oh, study – I'm a student.

**April:**   And what do you study?

**Jasvinder:**   I study biology. I'd like to be a scientist.

**April:**   Hmm. OK, and do you have a busy lifestyle?

**Jasvinder:**   Yes, I think so. I have a lot of homework.

**April:**   I see, OK, and how do you relax?

**Jasvinder:**   Hm. Well, I go to a gym. I do a lot of exercise.

**April:**   Really?

**Jasvinder:**   Yes. I feel happy when I do exercise.

**April:**   Yes, I know what you mean. And when do you go to the gym?

**Jasvinder:**   Oh, every day.

**April:**   Every day? Wow. OK, and what other things do you do to relax? Do you go to the cinema for example?

**Jasvinder:**   No, not really. I watch films on my laptop at home.

**April:**   I see. And what about your friends? When do you go out with them?

**Jasvinder:** Oh, well, I have some friends at the gym. But I also go out on Saturday afternoons. We go to a café and have a coffee and talk about ... well, we talk about life, people we know, that kind of thing.

**April:** I think I know what you mean! OK, so ...

 **3.8**

**1**

**Student A:** Do you watch TV in the evening?

**Student B:** No, not really. I go to the gym in the evening.

**2**

**Student C:** Do you cook food for your family?

**Student D:** No! I can order pizza but I can't cook!

**3**

**Student E:** Do you eat out at restaurants?

**Student F:** Yes. I go with my family every Monday evening.

**4**

**Student G:** Do you write a blog?

**Student H:** No, but I follow one. It's about football.

**5**

**Student I:** Which computer games do you play?

**Student J:** I like *NBA Basketball*. I play it on my PC.

**6**

**Student K:** How many texts do you send every day?

**Student L:** I'm not sure. I send a lot of them – 40 or 50, maybe?

 **3.9**

1 What food do you like?
2 Do you watch the news?
3 Do you read books?
4 What football team do you like?
5 Do you cook dinner in the evening?
6 Which bus do you take to school?

🔊 **3.10**

true; room; computer; good; would; pull

🔊 **3.11**

food; you; news; books; football; cook; school

# UNIT 4

▶ The Great Barrier Reef

The Great Barrier Reef is the Earth's largest living thing. It lies off the coast of Australia. The Great Barrier Reef started to grow about 10,000 years ago, and it is huge. It is made up of 900 islands. It is larger than Italy and it can be seen from space. The Great Barrier Reef is home to 400 kinds of coral and 1,600 kinds of fish. Fishing is not allowed here, but tourism is very popular. It is big business for Australia and brings in five billion dollars a year. People love seeing the different kinds of fish.

There are more species per cubic metre than in any other place on the planet; for example, more

fish varieties live on a single reef than in the entire Caribbean. And these are humpback whales that spend the winter here in the warm water. And there are sharks too. Small dog sharks and the great white on the Great Barrier Reef.

 **4.1**

1 Where is this?
2 What are these red circles?
3 The blue one here and the yellow one there.
4 Yes, that's a good example.
5 Those cities have a lot of important places.
6 The economy is good here.

🔊 **4.2**

**Lecturer:** Now, today I want to talk about megaregions. We're going to look at megaregions in different parts of the world, but first, we're going to look at this. Now, I have a map here. Where is this? Yes, Mehmet?

**Mehmet:** Europe. It's Europe at night.

**Lecturer:** Yes, yes, that's right. OK, so look at the map now. What are these red circles? Belis, yes.

**Belis:** Are they cities? I think that one's Istanbul. There, at 'G'.

**Lecturer:** Yes, that's right. These are big cities. Um, here we have London at 'A', then here at 'C' is Paris and that one there at 'D' is Madrid. OK, now you see these two lines? The blue one here and the yellow one there? These show megaregions. Now, what does 'mega' mean?

**Belis:** Um, *mega* means 'big', 'very big'.

**Lecturer:** Yes, that's right. Thank you, Belis. So can you give me an example of a mega*city*?

**Mehmet:** Istanbul.

**Lecturer:** Yes, Istanbul.

**Mehmet:** Er, Shanghai.

**Lecturer:** Yes, that's a good example. OK, so a megacity is a big city but a megaregion is a group of important cities. They're important for business and they're important because a lot of people live there.

We sometimes call this blue line here the 'blue banana'. It's the name for a group of cities that go from north to south in Europe. Those cities have a lot of important places. For example, ports, airports and big banks. Rotterdam is a good example. The economy is good here. That's at 'B', here on the map. It has a very busy port.

This yellow line that goes from East to West is another megaregion. It's also ...

 **4.3**

**1**

**Speaker 1:** Where's the supermarket? Is it near the bank?

**Speaker 2:** Yes, it's behind the bank.

**2**

**Speaker 3:**  Is there a hotel near here?

**Speaker 4:**  Yes. There's one next to the train station.

**3**

**Speaker 5:**  Where's the Blue Mosque? Is it in Cairo?

**Speaker 6:**  No. It's in the old town of Istanbul.

**4**

**Speaker 7:**  Excuse me, where's the library?

**Speaker 8:**  It's opposite the restaurant on Tower Street.

**5**

**Speaker 9:**  I can't find the restaurant – is it near here?

**Speaker 10:**  Yes, it's between the bank and the bookshop.

**6**

**Speaker 11:**  Where's the train station?

**Speaker 12:**  It's in front of that big clock. There – on the right.

**7**

**Speaker 13:**  Where can I get a bus?

**Speaker 14:**  At the bus stop over there. Can you see it?

**8**

**Speaker 15:**  I'm looking for the park. Is it near the bridge?

**Speaker 16:**  No. It's there on the left. It's behind that school.

🔊 **4.4**

**Kerry:**  ... OK then, so we're at the clock and that means it's the end of today's tour of the university campus. So, any questions? No? OK, so can you remember – what are we going to do now? Faisal?

**Faisal:**  Um, take a quiz? About the places in the university?

**Kerry:**  Yes, that's right!

**Students:**  *[groaning]*

**Kerry:**  Oh, come on, guys! There's a lot of information in your first week at university. I don't want you to get lost! OK, so, Faisal, Takashi and Abdullah – you're Team A. And Akira, Katsuo and Ahmed – you're Team B. Now – I ask the questions, and you get one point for a correct answer. OK?

**Students:**  Yes. / Yes. / Yeah.

**Kerry:**  Right then. Question one. Where's the train station? Yes! Katsuo!

**Katsuo:**  It's opposite the International Business School.

**Kerry:**  OK, and how do I get there from here?

**Katsuo:**  Go along Leeds Street ...

**Kerry:**  Uh-huh.

**Katsuo:**  Then go over the bridge.

**Kerry:**  Excellent! One point to Team B. OK, two. How do I get to the supermarket from here? Yes! Ahmed.

**Ahmed:**  Em, OK, you can go along South Road and then turn left.

**Kerry:**  Turn left where?

**Ahmed:**  At the Chemistry building on Kroto Street. Go along Kroto Street and over the bridge on Canal Street. The supermarket is on the right, next to the bus station.

**Kerry:**  Perfect! Another point to Team B. Right then. Next question. Can you tell me the way to the library? Yes! Takashi!

**Takashi:**  Yes, go through Clock Tower Garden to the Student's Union. Then turn right ...

**Kerry:**  Uh-huh.

**Takashi:**  ... then turn left. The university library is behind the student's union on Park Street West.

**Kerry:**  Is that East or West?

**Takashi:**  West.

**Kerry:**  Correct! You guys are brilliant. OK, now. Four. Is there a bank near here?

**Faisal:**  Yes!

**Kerry:**  OK, Faisal.

**Faisal:**  It's behind the Business School. Go along Leeds Street and then turn left. Go along Hospital Road and turn left. There are three buildings on York Street. The bank is next to the café and opposite the gym on South Road.

**Kerry:**  Great! That's right. OK, Five. Where's the Physics ...

🔊 **4.5**

**1**  Where's the gym?

**2**  Is there a café near here?

**3**  How do I get to the language centre?

**4**  Can you tell me the way to the train station?

**5**  I'm looking for the library. Is it near here?

🔊 **4.6**

**a**  Excuse me! Can you tell me the way to the train station, please?

**b**  Excuse me! I think I'm lost. Is there a café near here?

**c**  Excuse me! How do I get to the Language Centre?

🔊 **4.7**

**1**  Excuse me! ...

Where's the ...

... bank, please?

Excuse me! Where's the bank, please?

**2**  Excuse me! ...

I think I'm lost.

How do I get to ...

... the gym?

Excuse me! I think I'm lost. How do I get to the gym?

**3**  Excuse me! ...

Can you tell me ...

... the way to ...

... the café?

Excuse me! Can you tell me the way to the café?

**4.8**

1 It's opposite the International Business School.
2 It's in the old town of Istanbul.
3 Go through Clock Tower Garden to the Student's Union.
4 It's in front of that big clock. There – on the right.
5 OK then, so we're at the clock.
6 Go along Leeds Street. Then go over the bridge.
7 There's one next to the train station.
8 It's there on the left. It's behind that school.

# UNIT 5

## ▶ Free diving

Europe. Italy. The island of Sicily. Sicily is the biggest island in the Mediterranean Sea. Today, it is home to five million people. Sicily has many old traditions. One of Sicily's oldest traditions is fishing. Today, there are not many jobs for fishermen in Sicily. Meet 24-year-old Sicilian, Michaele Ralo. Michaele wants to be a free diver. Free diving is when you dive without oxygen tanks. Free diving is a modern sport, but it is also an ancient tradition in Sicily.

Michaele trains every day. Each time he dives, he swims faster, dives deeper and stays under water longer. He is training for a competition but also because he wants to be a professional diver. To become a professional, Michaele must dive to more than 50 metres. Free diving is a dangerous sport.

Today, there is a free-diving competition. The town wakes up to a beautiful morning.

Fans come to wish Michaele good luck. The divers go out to sea. Safety divers go down before the free divers to help in an emergency. Then it's time! The older divers go first. They dive deep and stay down for four minutes. These divers are good. They are better than the others that Michaele knows. Michaele waits for his turn. He sees the dive in his mind, going faster and deeper. He's off! It's a good start, swimming fast and deep. It's a long dive. The older men are worried. But Michaele returns. He's happy. He knows it's a good dive. The dive is over 56 metres – Michaele can become a professional!

**5.1**

1 /k/ ... quick   2 /ng/ ... strong   3 /f/ ... tough

**5.2**

Country; evening; father; mosque; phone; physics; singer; smoke; spring

**5.3**

Running's a tough sport.
Free diving's tougher than running.
Mark's a strong man.
Lisa's stronger than Steph.
Yoga's good for you.
Yoga's better for you than tae kwon do.

**5.4**

**Professor:** Now, uh, good morning, everybody. For this morning's lecture, we have with us Doctor Kate Hunter. She's an expert in sports science and today she's going to talk to us about men, women and sport. That's right, isn't it?

**Dr Hunter:** Yes, yes, that's correct.

**Professor:** OK, so please can we welcome Doctor Hunter.

**Dr Hunter:** Thank you, thank you. Can I just say that I'm very happy to be here with you this morning. I want to start with this question: Are men better than women in all sports?

Many people say 'Yes'. But is it true? Are they correct? And how do they know it's true? Many of my students, my male students that is, say 'Men are bigger and stronger than women. They are tougher and they can run faster – they must be better!'

But these are opinions, not facts. There are in fact sports that women can do better than men. And this morning, I'm going to tell you about five of them.

Women have stronger backs than men. Look at this photograph of a woman's lower back. Women have three bones here but men have only two. This means that yoga is easier for women.

OK, OK, there are some of you that think yoga isn't a sport. So let's look at the next photograph.

Ah, tae kwon do! My favourite sport! Now, my research shows that women are better than men at tae kwon do. 'How?' I hear you ask. Well, women learn quicker than men. They are also faster. So, it's true that men are bigger and stronger, but they are not better than women in this sport.

**Student:** But Doctor Hunter! Please can I ask you ...

**5.5**

**Teacher:** ... OK, thank you, Sara. Very interesting! Now! Who's next?

**Alma:** It's me.

**Teacher:** Ah, yes, Alma. OK and you're going to talk about ... ?

**Alma:** I'm going to compare two kinds of sport. Well, two kinds of exercise.

**Teacher:** Yes, I remember now! Good, good. OK, so please go ahead.

**Alma:** Thank you. OK, good afternoon, everybody! Today, many young people have an unhealthy lifestyle and this means they can be unhappy. This is a real problem.

So I want to start with this question: How can we make young people fitter? How can we make them healthier? Happier?

Here's one answer. Well, in fact, here are *two* answers. Pilates and zumba. These are two very good kinds of exercise. They are more popular with women than men, but men can also do them.

Now, why are they good for you? And are they the same or different? Well, they are different for sure. Zumba is faster than pilates and, I think, people enjoy zumba more. There is music, you can dance with your friends, have a good time ... all very good. But is it better than pilates?

We-e-ll ... no. Pilates *is* slower than zumba. That's true. But it's not a problem. In fact, it means that it's better for older people. Zumba is better for your heart and you can lose more weight. But pilates is good for your bones and muscles. That means it can make you stronger. Now, let's look at ...

🔊 5.6

1   Basketball is faster than football.
2   But is basketball better than football?
3   A football team is bigger than a basketball team.
4   Judo is better for young men.
5   Tennis is better for young women.

🔊 5.7

OK, good afternoon, everybody! Today, many young people have an unhealthy lifestyle and this means they can be unhappy. This is a real problem. So I want to start with this question: How can we make young people fitter? How can we make them healthier? Happier?

🔊 5.8

OK, good morning, everybody! Today, I want to talk to you about three kinds of exercise. I want to start with this question: Which sport is better for young men? Which is better for women?

# UNIT 6

▶ Fire rangers

In a forest in Minnesota, a fire starts and quickly spreads. At the Minnesota Fire Centre, Mary Locke takes the call and the fire rangers go into action. The helicopter crew sends information about the fire back to the Fire Centre. And then it's the turn of the crew of the CL2-15 to take off. The CL2-15 is no ordinary plane. It is a fire-fighting plane. The pilots have to be very experienced. They are going to pick up water from this lake. It can be a dangerous job. The CL2-15 is flying at 140 kilometres per hour now. The pilot must be very careful. If he makes a mistake, the plane will crash. It's time to open the water tanks on the plane. The plane picks up water from the lake. This is the most dangerous time for the crew. But the pilot does his job and picks up more than 5,000 litres of water. Then it's time to put out the fire.

The pilot has to fly low over the trees to hit the fire. He also needs to make the ground wet in front of the fire so it can't spread. The water drops on the fire. It's a good hit! But the fire is a big one – the fire rangers have to go back to the lake. In just two minutes, the plane is ready again. The crew have to drop water 20 times to put out the fire. At last, it's time for the fire rangers to go home ... until the next time.

🔊 6.1

lawyer; banker; engineer; pilot; musician; scientist

🔊 6.2

**a**

**A:**   Can I help you?

**B:**   Yes. I want to speak good English. What should I do?

**A:**   I think you should learn five new words every day.

**B:**   Good idea!

**b**

**A:**   Hello, Philip. How can I help you?

**B:**   Well, I want to study a foreign language. But I don't know what to do. Should I study Turkish? Or German? Or Chinese?

**A:**   Well, I don't think you should study German or Chinese. Your father has a business in Istanbul. So I think you should study Turkish.

**B:**   That's great, thanks!

🔊 6.3

What should I do?

Should I study Turkish?

You should work hard.

I think you should watch videos in English.

I don't think you should drink a lot of coffee.

🔊 6.4

**Lisa:**   Come in!

**Miriam:**   Hello! It's, uh, I'm Miriam.

**Lisa:**   Ah yes, Miriam! Please, come in. Take a seat.

**Miriam:**   Thank you.

**Lisa:**   So, how can I help you?

**Miriam:**   Well, I'm going to college next year.

**Lisa:**   Uh-huh.

**Miriam:**   I have to choose a course ... but I don't know what to do. Should I go to medical school or should I go to music school? Should I be a doctor? A musician? Should I go to law school and become a lawyer?

**Lisa:**   Hmm. Those are good questions. Tell me about music school.

**Miriam:**   Well, there aren't many jobs for musicians. Well, OK, I'm sorry. That's not true. There *are* a lot of jobs in music – but it's a hard life. They work hard, but many musicians don't earn a lot of money.

**Lisa:**   I see. And what about medical school?

**Miriam:**   Well, a doctor's life ... Wow! It's a good job. It's not boring and you can earn good money *and* help people.

**Lisa:**   Yes, that's true.

**Miriam:**   But ... I don't know. Medical school's difficult. You have to work hard.

**Lisa:**   Hm. What do your parents say?

**Miriam:**   Well, my mother thinks I should go to medical school.

**Lisa:**   Why?

**Miriam:** Oh, because my grades are good. I have good grades in science and English.

**Lisa:** And what about your father?

**Miriam:** Well, he says I can be a doctor or a lawyer or, well, anything I guess. What do you think? What should I do?

**Lisa:** Well, you're a good student and you have good grades. But for now, I think you should get a job.

**Miriam:** What? Why?

**Lisa:** Well, I don't think you should go to university now because you don't know if you want to be a musician or a doctor ... or a lawyer! I think you should get a job. Then you can go to university later when you know what ...

 6.5

**Paul:** Morning, Emma! And how are you today?

**Emma:** I'm fine thanks, Paul.

**Paul:** Good, good. Now then – what do you have for me here?

**Emma:** Well, here are two people for the job at the Sports Centre.

**Paul:** I see. Which job is this? Is it for the fitness instructor? Or for the sports-centre nurse?

**Emma:** This is for the fitness instructor. We're going to look at people for the nurse's job next week.

**Paul:** Ah, next week, OK, I see. So, who's this?

**Emma:** Well, this is Alan Green.

**Paul:** Ah, I see he's an American.

**Emma:** Yes. What do you think?

**Paul:** Well, he's fit and strong ... and he does a lot of sport. Football, basketball, karate, judo. That's great.

**Emma:** But ...?

**Paul:** But, he's a student. I think a good fitness instructor should be a good teacher. I want a person who has experience, a person who can teach me tennis or volleyball.

**Emma:** OK, well, here's Lucy Lau.

**Paul:** Hmm. Ah good! She's a sports scientist ... and she's a fitness instructor! That's great! So, I think Lucy is our new fitness instructor. What do you think?

**Emma:** Well ...

**Paul:** You're not sure?

**Emma:** Lucy is very good. But I think a fitness instructor has to be fit and strong. I think he – or she – has to be a good example for the students.

**Paul:** Interesting, go on.

**Emma:** We want a person who can make the students work hard. Lucy says 'it is important to be kind and polite'. That's a good idea. But if you want to be fit, you have to work hard. I think Alan can help people do that.

**Paul:** I see, I see. But I think we should choose Lucy. She teaches zumba, pilates and yoga – and these are very popular right now.

**Emma:** Mm, that's true. Would you like me to write to Lucy and tell her the good news?

**Paul:** Yes, I think that would be ...

 6.6

1 Fatima has two jobs.
2 Mehmet has to work very hard.
3 I have a very good job.
4 Engineers have a difficult job.
5 Paul has an important job.
6 Builders have to work fast.
7 Emma has to choose a new fitness instructor.
8 Lawyers have to be clever.

# UNIT 7

## ▶ Homes in Dharavi, India

Today, Mumbai in India is an international centre. The number of people who live there has grown a lot. Many of these people live in slums. For example, the Dharavi Slum, where over one million people live in an area smaller than two square kilometres. It is home to more people than any other place on the planet. The number of homes in the slum grew and grew. In the small streets of the slum, there is a whole city. A lot of small businesses, shops and schools can be found in the spaces between the houses. The businesses in Dharavi earn 350 million dollars a year.

Krishna has his own business. He sells satellite TV to the people in Dharavi. Krishna has so many contacts in Dharavi that he has become an important person in the community. Today he is visiting a family. Sushila, her husband and three children all live and eat in this very small space. Every year, when there is a lot of rain during the monsoon, their home becomes full of water. To stop these problems, the family has decided to pull down their home and build a new one. Krishna has many people building the new house. Some weeks later, the walls are finished, so the painting can now begin. Krishna asks Sushila's family to see their new home. They are very pleased with the work and soon start to make it look like a home again.

 7.1

1 an author of many books
2 I help architects.
3 For example
4 good ideas
5 restaurants in London
6 What about England?

🔊 7.2

**Paul:** Good evening. I'm Paul Clark, and welcome to 'Mind'. I have a special guest today – Dr Kay Thompson. Dr Thompson is a psychologist and an author of many books. Welcome, Dr Thompson. Now, you're *not* an architect, but you help design buildings. What do you do?

**Dr Thompson:** Well, I help architects choose good colours for their buildings.

**Paul:** Is colour important?

**Dr Thompson:**   Yes. Very important. Why? Because colour can change the way we think, the way we feel, even the way we talk.

**Paul:**   Really?

**Dr Thompson:**   Yes. For example, many restaurants in Mexico have orange walls.

**Paul:**   Why?

**Dr Thompson:**   Well, what do you think?

**Paul:**   Oh, um, I don't know, er, is orange a warm colour? Is it a friendly colour?

**Dr Thompson:**   Those are good ideas. But no. The walls are orange because some experts think that orange makes people feel hungry.

**Paul:**   Hungry? How interesting! But ... is that true? You don't see many orange restaurants in London, for example. Why is that?

**Dr Thompson:**   Because colours mean different things in different countries. For example, if you go on the internet and look for photographs of 'Chinese restaurants', you're going to see a lot of red!

**Paul:**   Why? Do they think that red makes people feel hungry?

**Dr Thompson:**   Good question, but no. Many Chinese restaurants are red because in China red is the colour of fire, of happiness and of all the good things in life.

**Paul:**   I see. This is really interesting. So what about England? If my friend opens a restaurant, what colour should it be?

**Dr Thompson:**   Well, if you mean traditional English food, white is a good colour. White and also a wood colour.

**Paul:**   Oh? Why?

**Dr Thompson:**   Because natural things are important to many people in England. White means fresh and clean, and the wood colours – brown, yellow – are natural. And nature is healthy.

**Paul:**   I see, so what I ...

 **7.3**

**Dale:**   ... thanks for the coffee, Hakan! Very nice!

**Hakan:**   Yes, it's good Turkish coffee. OK then, shall we start?

**Dale:**   Yes, I think so. OK, so we need a place for our new office. What about here?

**Hakan:**   Where?

**Dale:**   The town centre. What do you think?

**Hakan:**   Well, it's a good place. It's near some good roads. But ... I don't think we should go there.

**Dale:**   Oh? Why not?

**Hakan:**   Because the buildings in the town centre are very old. They are cold in winter and hot in summer. They're not comfortable places.

**Dale:**   Oh, I see. That's not good.

**Hakan:**   No. And the buildings there are expensive.

**Dale:**   Really?

**Hakan:**   Yes. My sister's a lawyer, and her office is in the town centre. She likes her job but she does *not* like her building.

**Dale:**   OK, so not there, then! Hm. What about here?

**Hakan:**   The park?

**Dale:**   Yes. It's quiet and it's not far from a big road. What do you think?

**Hakan:**   Hm, I'm not sure. It's quite far from the town. What about here? Near the train station?

**Dale:**   The train station is good. It's good for travel ... but I think we should go to the park. The buildings near the train station aren't cheap.

**Hakan:**   They're not?

**Dale:**   No. They're quite expensive.

**Hakan:**   OK, let's go with the park. I'm happy with that. Now what about the design? I think we should have big windows. What about you?

**Dale:**   Yes, I agree. Big windows are good. What about the walls? What colour do you think we should paint the walls?

**Hakan:**   Hmm. What about blue?

**Dale:**   Blue's a good colour, but I'm not sure. Blue can make people feel cold.

**Hakan:**   Ah yes, that's true. What about yellow? Because it's a warm and sunny colour.

**Dale:**   Yes, You're right. Yellow's a good colour. OK, so what's next? Ah, OK, furniture. So what do you ...

 **7.4**

**1**

**Dale:**   OK, so we need a place for our new office. What about here?

**Hakan:**   Where?

**Dale:**   The town centre. What do you think?

**Hakan:**   Well, it's a good place. It's near some good roads. But ... I don't think we should go there.

**Dale:**   Oh? Why not?

**Hakan:**   Because the buildings in the town centre are very old. They are cold in winter and hot in summer. They're not comfortable places.

**2**

**Dale:**   What about here?

**Hakan:**   The park?

**Dale:**   Yes. It's quiet and it's not far from a big road. What do you think?

**Hakan:**   Hm, I'm not sure. It's quite far from the town. What about here? Near the train station?

**Dale:**   The train station is good. It's good for travel ... but I think we should go to the park. The buildings near the train station aren't cheap.

**3**

**Hakan:**   Now what about the design? I think we should have big windows. What about you?

**Dale:**   Yes, I agree. Big windows are good.

# UNIT 8

 Chinese food

China is famous all over the world for its food. And in its capital city, Beijing, you can find many night markets where they cook chicken, duck, vegetables and noodles.

China has many traditional dishes. Chinese people love to eat together in restaurants.

When they cook at home, Chinese people like to eat a lot of vegetables. They fry them quickly in different sauces. The most popular Chinese food is rice.

These people are planting rice in the mountains. A quarter of the world's rice comes from China. These fields were made 500 years ago and they are still growing rice here today. It is difficult to use machines in the rice fields, so the farmers use animals to help them. They collect and then dry the rice and then it is ready to cook. Chinese people steam the rice until it is hot and sticky. Family meals are important and everybody enjoys chatting and eating together.

🔊 8.1

**1**

**Speaker 1:** Is the population there about seventy million?

**Speaker 2:** Um, no, I think it's about seventeen.

**Speaker 1:** Seventeen million? OK, thanks.

**2**

**Speaker 3:** We feed sixty children from poor families here.

**Speaker 4:** Sorry, how many children? Sixteen?

**Speaker 3:** No, sixty.

**3**

**Speaker 5:** Thirteen per cent of this class are vegetarians – people who don't eat meat.

**Speaker 6:** Thirty? Are you sure?

**Speaker 5:** No, no – thirteen!

**4**

**Speaker 7:** People in this city eat fifteen thousand tonnes of beef every month.

**Speaker 8:** Is that true? Fifty thousand tonnes every month?

**Speaker 7:** No, fifteen thousand – not fifty.

🔊 8.2

**O'Connor:** Thank you, thank you, everyone. Well, let's start, shall we? In my lecture tonight, I want to answer this question: 'How do we feed a city?' The question is easy, but the answer is difficult. And it's an important question.

Why? Well, there are four important facts about cities that you have to know.

First, cities don't have farms. True, some people have gardens and they can grow vegetables, fruit, etc. But not many people can do this.

There are many more people who can't grow their own food. So they have to buy it from supermarkets, from restaurants, etc.

Secondly, people in cities are richer than people in the country. True, there are poor people in cities; sometimes a lot of poor people. But there are many people that have money, and these people eat a lot of meat. They eat more lamb, more beef and more chicken than people in the country.

This is a big problem. Before we can eat meat, we have to feed the animals. This means that food for people becomes food for animals. And that means that food becomes expensive – rice, bread, vegetables – they all become more expensive.

In some countries, poor people spend more than sixty per cent of their money on food.

Thirdly, modern cities are big and they are becoming bigger. Today, 30 cities have a population of more than ten million people. In 2045, we are going to have more than *50* cities with a population of 20 million people ... that's *20* million. Twenty.

And the last fact. More than half the people in the world live in cities. In 2045, 75 per cent of people are going to live in cities. More people and more cities means bigger problems.

So! What can we do about this? Well, I'm going to ...

 8.3

**Sofia:** Hello! I'm Sofia. This afternoon, I'm going to tell you about the results of my survey. There were 20 students in my survey. My questions were on the topic of 'Food and culture'. I think this is an interesting topic. For example, I'm from Italy, and food is very important in my country and in my culture.

OK, so my first question was 'Where are you from?' and here are the results. You can see here that 50% of students come from England and 15% come from Spain. 20% of students come from Italy, like me, and 15% of students come from Egypt. So you can see that half of the students are from England.

OK, my second question was 'Is food important in your culture?'. The answers are interesting. You can see here that 'yes' is 70% and 'no' is 30%. That's six people! I was very surprised!

My third question was 'Are family meals important?'. That is, is it important to eat with your family? Again, I was very surprised because again 'yes' is 70% and 'no' is 30%.

My last question was 'Why are family meals important?'. You can see here that the results are interesting. There were two answers to this question.

First, 80% of people think family meals are a good place to talk. They think it's a good time for parents to see their children. Secondly, 20% of people think family meals are cheaper and healthier. They think that families cook fresh food and don't eat fast food.

So my conclusion is that food is important in families and families are important in culture. Thank you! Any questions?

🔊 **8.4**

**Sofia:** Hello! I'm Sofia. This afternoon, I'm going to tell you about the results of my survey. There were 20 students in my survey. My questions were on the topic of 'Food and culture'. I think this is an interesting topic.

🔊 **8.5**

**Tomoko:** Good morning! I'm Tomoko. I'm going to tell you about the results of my survey. There were 34 students in my survey. My topic was 'traditional Japanese food'. I think this is an interesting topic.

**Ahmed:** Hello, everybody! I'm Ahmed. I'm going to tell you about the results of my survey. My topic was 'fast food in Abu Dhabi'. There were 50 students in my survey. I think this is a good topic.

🔊 **8.6**

1 I'm going to tell you about the results of my survey.
2 There were 15 students in my survey.
3 My topic was food and culture.

🔊 **8.7**

1 OK, so, my first question was 'Where are you from?'.
2 So you can see that half of the students are from England.
3 OK, my second question was 'Is food important in your culture?'.
4 The answers are interesting.
5 You can see here that 'yes' is 70% and 'no' is 30%!
6 My third question was 'Are family meals important?'.
7 My last question was 'Why are family meals important?'.
8 There were two answers to this question.

# UNIT 9

## ▶ Animals and people

Today, busy cities are everywhere, and people live in every part of the world.

But what about animals? Where do they live when people build their cities? Where do they go? To answer these questions, we're going to Nepal in Asia to look at two different animals. We are travelling from Darjeeling to the Kathmandu valley and then to Chitwan National Park. Our first animal lives in green forests. This is a red panda. It's a very rare animal. Some people say there are only 10,000 red pandas in the wild. Red pandas are rare because people hunt them or because cities are getting bigger and they have nowhere to live. At night, the red pandas come down from the trees to eat. They eat leaves, flowers, eggs and fruit. In the morning, they return to the trees to sleep. They can fall out of the trees when they sleep, so it's important to find a good branch. The forest is the red panda's world. They can't live in cities like this. But the red panda is safe because no one can hunt them there. Let's look at another animal in a different part of the Chitwan National Park.

Look at the river. That's not a branch in the water – it's a one-horned Asiatic rhino. Rhinos often relax in the river on a hot day. Rhinos are dangerous animals – they can kill people easily. But in fact, there are now only 3,000 of these animals in India. Hunters look for rhinos. They kill them for their horns. A hunter can sell a rhino horn for 100,000 dollars or more. But these rhinos here are safe because they are protected in Chitwan National Park. The government in India sends police and soldiers to look after the rhinos. People can be a problem for animals – but we also look after them.

🔊 **9.1**

hands; brains; climb; world; wild; ground; umbrella

🔊 **9.2**

**Presenter:** In half an hour, in 'Technology Today', we look at hovercraft in Alaska. But first, here's Kate Brand in our series on the animal world. In this week's 'Going Wild', Kate travels to Indonesia to meet some very special animals.

**Kate:** Now, it's noisy today because I'm in a jungle. I'm in the jungle in West Sumatra in Indonesia, and I'm here with Zaskia Basuki. Zaskia is a scientist and she knows a lot about the animal we're here to see today – the orangutan. So, Zaskia, what can you tell us?

**Zaskia:** Well, Kate, let me start with the name. In Indonesia and Malaysia, the word *orang* means 'man', and the word *hutan* means 'forest'. So 'orangutan' means 'the man in the forest'.

**Kate:** I see!

**Zaskia:** It's a good name for them, because orangutans are 'arboreal'. That means they live in trees. Here in Sumatra, they only walk on the ground when they have to. In fact, 90% of their life is in the trees. They're omnivores, so they can eat meat, fruit and vegetables, but they usually eat fruit. They're primates so—

**Kate:** Sorry, Zaskia …

**Zaskia:** No, no, that's OK.

**Kate:** For the listeners at home, can you just explain 'primate'?

**Zaskia:** Ah, yes, well, a primate is a kind of animal that can use its hands to climb trees. Primates usually have a big brain, too.

**Kate:** Really? So are orangutans clever?

**Zaskia:** Yes, yes, they are very clever. They are good toolmakers. That means they can make things to help them. For example, they can use sticks to find food or leaves to make an umbrella. There's a famous video of one orangutan in the rain. He's very wet, so he uses some leaves to make a big umbrella.

**Kate:** That's great!

**Zaskia:** Yes, so they …

**9.3**

**Jason:** Hi! How are you today? Good? Good! OK, good morning! I'm Jason, and today I'm going to tell you about a bird from my country – the American bald eagle. OK, so, where do they live? Well, you can see them in the US and Canada and here's a photograph of one.

You can see here that this bird is flying to its nest. 'Nest' is the name for the place where the eagle lives. Some nests can be very big. How big can they be? Well, there was one eagle's nest that was more than 1,000 kilos!

Here's another photograph. You can see she has these white feathers on her head.

So what do bald eagles eat? Well, fish are their prey. That means the eagles hunt them. And you see her yellow beak here? That beak is very sharp. That means it can cut the fish very easily.

OK, uh, and now Khaled is going to talk about an animal from his country.

**Khaled:** OK, good morning, everybody. My name's Khaled and I'm going to talk about the animal in this photograph here. So this is an Arabian oryx.

An oryx is a kind of wild animal that lives in the desert. You can see them in many countries in the Arab world. For example, Oman, Jordan, Saudi Arabia and near my home in Abu Dhabi.

They are famous for their horns. That's these two long, hard things on their head. You can see their horns better in this photograph. The horns are very sharp! Oryx can run and jump very fast. Oryx eat grass and also fruit when they can find it.

The oryx are nomadic. That means they do not live in one place in the desert, but they travel around.

Thank you! Now, I think …

**9.4**

1 OK, good morning! I'm Jason, and today I'm going to tell you about a bird from my country – the American bald eagle.

2 OK, good morning, everybody. My name's Khaled and I'm going to talk about the animal in this photograph here. So this is an Arabian oryx.

**9.5**

1 OK, so where do they live? Well, you can see them in the US and Canada, and here's a photograph of one.

2 Some nests can be very big. How big can they be? Well, there was one eagle's nest that was more than 1,000 kilos!

3 So what do bald eagles eat? Well, fish are their prey. That means the eagles hunt them.

**9.6**

**Luo Yan:** OK, hello, everybody. My name's Luo Yan, and I'm going to talk about brown bears. This is a photograph of a brown bear.

So, where do these bears live? Well, they live in forests and near rivers. They often live in mountains.

And where can you see brown bears? In a lot of countries! Brown bears live in America and Europe and parts of Asia.

How do they live? Well, they sleep for the winter and they hunt in the summer. They have to eat a lot in the summer, so bears are often hungry.

And so *what* do they eat? Well, they eat a lot of different things. They like fruit, fish, vegetables, nuts and grass.

So why are they special? Well, they are very, very strong animals. They can move rocks and trees and other big things easily.

# UNIT 10

## ▶ Alaskan transport

About 100 kilometres from the Arctic Circle is a village in Alaska. There are no roads in or out of town. In winter, the rivers are frozen and the ice is thin. Parts of the Tozitna River are less than five centimetres thick. Stan and Joey need to cross the river. Stan tests the ice to see if he can stand on it. The ice is very thin in places. The ice breaks. But Stan is safe. Stan and Joey hope that the dogs will run and jump over the hole in the ice. They are safe for now.

This is not the only kind of transport in Alaska, but other transport cannot travel over the ice. In another part of Alaska is the main town, called Bethel. All the supplies for the villages come through this town. These supplies are for the village of Akiachak. Akiachak is about 50 kilometres from Bethel. But there are no roads there. There is only one way to get to Akiachak – by hovercraft. When it is minus 40 degrees, boats and planes are useless. Over snow, ice and water, the hovercraft will follow the frozen river to Akiachak. Only the hovercraft can carry supplies. The hovercraft can travel over thin ice. The hovercraft arrives.

**10.1**

1238; 1868; 1923; 1996; 2005; 2015

**10.2**

1435; 1749; 1949; 1953; 2015

**10.3**

**Steve:** Hi! Good morning! Thank you for asking me here today. OK, so my name's Steve and I work for Transport for London. Today I'm going to tell you about the work we do and especially tell you about the electronic tickets we use in London.

OK, so what do we do at Transport for London? Well, we look after travellers in London. This can be people who travel in private transport or public transport. Three million people travel in private cars and taxis and another five million use the bus, trains and, of course, the famous London Underground – the world's oldest underground train network. So that's a total of around eight million people.

**Student:**    How old is it?

**Steve:**    Sorry? What was that?

**Student:**    How old is the London Underground?

**Steve:**    Ah! Oh, uh it's more than 150 years old. It opened in 1863.

**Student:**    Thanks.

**Steve:**    That's OK. So, Transport for London started in 2000, and in 2003 we introduced the Oyster card system of electronic tickets. Before Oyster cards, people had to buy paper tickets. And that was OK when fewer people lived and worked in London. They could buy tickets for one journey, or for a day or for a month. But there was a problem – it was very slow.

**Student:**    Why, how did people use tickets before?

**Steve:**    Each passenger waited to buy a ticket and then they went to the gate. At the gate, they put the ticket into the machine, then the gate opened and then they took their ticket from the machine. Now, this wasn't difficult, but it took a long time, and more people started to live and work in London, so we wanted a better kind of ticket.

So what did we do? We needed a faster ticket system, and this was the Oyster card. It's an electronic ticket and it's very easy to use. You can pay for your journeys online and you can walk through the gates much faster.

It's a great way …

🔊 **10.4**

**Teacher:**    OK, so work with your partner. Five minutes!

**Iman:**    Hi, hello. I'm sorry, what's your name?

**Anna:**    Oh, I'm Anna.

**Iman:**    Anna? OK, and I'm Iman. Can I go first?

**Anna:**    Yes, sure. What's your topic?

**Iman:**    Transport in cities: problems and solutions. OK, so I'm going to start with some facts about life in cities. The population of cities grows more quickly than in the countryside. This means that cities become really congested. This is because everyone uses cars to travel around the city, and this can be a problem. For example, it takes a long time to get to your destination, so drivers need to use a lot of petrol, which is expensive and also causes pollution. What is more, being in a car for a long time can be dangerous because drivers suffer from tiredness. So, what is the solution?

Some countries said that bicycles would be a good idea and have free bicycles in the city for people to use. Another place where the government is working hard to improve the transport system is in Dubai. Firstly, the plan is to reduce traffic congestion

by making public transport better, so they have introduced more buses and bus routes and also built a metro railway. But the problem is that buses get stuck in traffic jams, and commuters still have to drive to metro stations. So the plan for the future is to make the metro system bigger by going underground – like the London Underground – and also to go over the city with sky trains like they have in Bangkok. Also, because it is very hot in Dubai, they will build air-conditioned sky bridges with travelators to connect the stations so that people can walk around easily and won't need to drive …

🔊 **10.5**

**Iman:**    The population of cities grows more quickly than in the countryside. This means that cities become really congested. This is because everyone uses cars to travel around the city, and this can be a problem. For example, it takes a long time to get to your destination, so drivers need to use a lot of petrol, …

🔊 **10.6**

**Anna:**    Ships are great for sending goods by river. Ships are cheaper and often cleaner than road transport. But ships have some problems. For example, when there are a lot of ships, rivers can become dirty.

🔊 **10.7**

**Anna:**    You can see in this photograph that this happened in Europe. A lot of companies used old ships. Old ships were cheaper, but they had some problems. For example, petrol came out of the ships and into the rivers. The petrol killed the fish. Fishermen were angry because they could not catch any fish.

🔊 **10.8**

happen**ed**; us**ed**; visit**ed**; guess**ed**; add**ed**; hat**ed**; ask**ed**; help**ed**; show**ed**; watch**ed**; chang**ed**; decid**ed**

🔊 **10.9**

So, was it a good solution? Well, that's a very interesting question! Why? Because the companies weren't happy that they had to clean the rivers. The old ships were cheap, but modern ships are expensive. And they didn't want to pay to clean the rivers.

But there was some good news. The fishermen are happier because the rivers are cleaner. That means there are more fish than before. I think it was a good solution.

# ACKNOWLEDGEMENTS

## Author acknowledgements

I'd like to say a big thank you to the many individuals who had a hand in helping to bring this project together - Barry, Brigit, Geneve, Catriona - but I would like to give special thanks to Caroline Thiriau for giving me this opportunity and especially to Kate Hansford for her help, support and patience which were absolutely invaluable throughout.
N.M.White

## Publisher acknowledgements

The publishers are extremely grateful to the following people and their students for reviewing and trialling this course during its development. The course has benefited hugely from your insightful comments and feedback.

Mr M.K. Adjibade, King Saud University, Saudi Arabia; Canan Aktug, Bursa Technical University, Turkey; Olwyn Alexander, Heriot Watt University, UK; Valerie Anisy, Damman University, Saudi Arabia; Anwar Al-Fetlawi, University of Sharjah, UAE; Laila Al-Qadhi, Kuwait University, Kuwait; Tahani Al-Taha, University of Dubai, UAE; Ozlem Atalay, Middle East Technical University, Turkey; Seda Merter Ataygul, Bursa Technical University Turkey; Harika Altug, Bogazici University, Turkey; Kwab Asare, University of Westminster, UK; Erdogan Bada, Cukurova University, Turkey; Cem Balcikanli, Gazi University, Turkey; Gaye Bayri, Anadolu University, Turkey; Meher Ben Lakhdar, Sohar University, Oman; Emma Biss, Girne American University, UK; Dogan Bulut, Meliksah University, Turkey; Sinem Bur, TED University, Turkey; Alison Chisholm, University of Sussex, UK; Dr. Panidnad Chulerk , Rangsit University, Thailand; Sedat Cilingir, Bilgi University, Istanbul, Turkey; Sarah Clark, Nottingham Trent International College, UK; Elaine Cockerham, Higher College of Technology, Muscat, Oman; Asli Derin, Bilgi University, Turkey; Steven Douglass, University of Sunderland, UK; Jacqueline Einer, Sabanci University, Turkey; Basak Erel, Anadolu University, Turkey; Hande Lena Erol, Piri Reis Maritime University, Turkey; Gulseren Eyuboglu, Ozyegin University, Turkey; Muge Gencer, Kemerburgaz University, Turkey; Jeff Gibbons, King Fahed University of Petroleum and Minerals, Saudi Arabia; Maxine Gilway, Bristol University, UK; Dr Christina Gitsaki, HCT, Dubai Men's College, UAE; Sam Fenwick, Sohar University, Oman; Peter Frey, International House, Doha, Qatar; Dr. Majid Gharawi and colleagues at the English Language Centre, Jazan University, Saudi Arabia; Neil Harris, Swansea University, UK; Vicki Hayden, College of the North Atlantic, Qatar; Ajarn Naratip Sharp Jindapitak, Prince of Songkla University, Hatyai, Thailand; Joud Jabri-Pickett, United Arab Emirates University, Al Ain, UAE; Aysel Kilic, Anadolu University, Turkey; Ali Kimav, Anadolu University, Turkey; Bahar Kiziltunali, Izmir University of Economics, Turkey; Kamil Koc, Ozel Kasimoglu Coskun Lisesi, Turkey; Ipek Korman-Tezcan, Yeditepe University, Turkey; Philip Lodge, Dubai Men's College, UAE; Iain Mackie, Al Rowdah University, Abu Dhabi, UAE; Katherine Mansfield, University of Westminster, UK; Kassim Mastan, King Saud University, Saudi Arabia; Elspeth McConnell, Newham College, UK; Lauriel Mehdi, American University of Sharjah, UAE; Dorando Mirkin-Dick, Bell International Institute, UK; Dr Sita Musigrungsi, Prince of Songkla University, Hatyai, Thailand; Mark Neville, Al Hosn University, Abu Dhabi, UAE; Shirley Norton, London School of English, UK; James Openshaw, British Study Centres, UK; Hale Ottolini, Mugla Sitki Kocman University, Turkey; David Palmer, University of Dubai, UAE; Michael Pazinas, United Arab Emirates University, UAE; Troy Priest, Zayed University, UAE; Alison Ramage Patterson, Jeddah, Saudi Arabia; Paul Rogers, Qatar Skills Academy, Qatar; Josh Round, Saint George International, UK; Harika Saglicak, Bogazici University, Turkey; Asli Saracoglu, Isik University, Turkey; Neil Sarkar, Ealing, Hammersmith and West London College, UK; Nancy Shepherd, Bahrain University, Bahrain; Jonathan Smith, Sabanci University, Turkey; Peter Smith, United Arab Emirates University, UAE; Adem Soruc, Fatih University Istanbul, Turkey; Dr Peter Stanfield, HCT, Madinat Zayed & Ruwais Colleges, UAE; Maria Agata Szczerbik, United Arab Emirates University, Al Ain, UAE; Burcu Tezcan-Unal, Bilgi University, Turkey; Dr Nakonthep Tipayasuparat, Rangsit University, Thailand; Scott Thornbury, The New School, New York, USA; Susan Toth, HCT, Dubai Men's Campus, Dubai, UAE; Melin Unal, Ege University, Izmir, Turkey; Aylin Unaldi, Bogaziçi University, Turkey; Colleen Wackrow, Princess Nourah bint Abdulrahman University, Riyadh, Saudi Arabia; Gordon Watts, Study Group, Brighton UK; Poh Leng Wendelkin, INTO Middlesex Street; Halime Yildiz, Bilkent University, Ankara, Turkey; Ferhat Yilmaz, Kahramanmaras Sutcu Imam University, Turkey.

Special thanks to Peter Lucantoni for sharing his expertise, both pedagogical and cultural.

## Text and Photo acknowledgements

The authors and publishers acknowledge the following sources of copyright material and are grateful for the permissions granted. While every effort has been made, it has not always been possible to identify the sources of all the material used, or to trace all copyright holders. If any omissions are brought to our notice, we will be happy to include the appropriate acknowledgements on reprinting.

p.12:(1) © Eric Limon/Shutterstock; p.12: (2) © szefai/Shutterstock; p.12: (3) © Steven Vidler/Eurasia Press/Corbis; p.14/15: © Stefano Rellandini/Reuters; p.18(L): © Young Wolff Photography; p.18(R): Jochen Schlenker/Corbis; p.20: © Tom Merton/Getty Images; p.23(a): © Paul Seheult/Eye Ubiquitous; p.23(b): © Zelig Shaul/Rex Features; p.23(c): Ramin Talaie/Corbis; p.23(d,e,f): Getty Images; pp.32/33: © Weatherstock/Corbis; p.37, 38(L): © Alan Haynes/Alamy; p.37, 38(C): © Cliff Hyde Stock/Alamy; p.37, 38(R): © Stuart Abraham/ Alamy; p.41(L): © Ken Brown/Getty; p.41(R),42: © Paul H Kuiper/Corbis; p.41(B): © Tim Graham/Alamy; p.44(L): © Amana Images/Alamy; p.44(R): © Benjamin Torode/Getty; pp.50/51: © Scott Stulbeg/Corbis; p.54(L): © Bon Appetit/Alamy; p.54(R): Fuse/Getty; p.57: USB70/Alamy; p.59: MBI/Alamy; pp.68/69: Horizons Wild/Alamy; p.70(L): © Stephen Frink/Getty; p.70(R): © Robert Yin/Corbis; p.70(BL): © Danita Delimont/Getty; p.70(BR): PM Images/Getty; p.73: © Deco/Alamy; p.75: © Peter Adams/Getty; pp.86/87: © Eric Augenstein/Corbis; p.90(L): © RedChopSticks/Getty; p.90(C): © Edvard March/Corbis; p.90(R): © Enigma/Alamy; p.94(a): © Lightpoet/Shutterstock; p.94(b): © Rafael Ben-Ari/Xinhau Press/Corbis; p.94(c): © OJO Images/ Getty; p.94(d): © Jurgen Hasenkopf/Alamy; p.94(e): Brian Fitzgerald/Aurora Photos/Corbis; p.96(TL): © Getty; p.96(BL): Sports Illustrated/Getty; p.96(TR): © Rod Walker/Getty; p.96(BR): AFP/Getty; p.101: © Dmitry Kalinovsky/ Shutterstock; pp.104/105: © Purestock/Alamy; p.117: Dream Pictures/Corbis; p.118(T): © Steve Hix/Somos Images/Corbis; p.118(B): © Susan Vogel/ Getty; pp.122/123: © Peter Adams/Getty; p.129(a): Glow Images RM/Alamy; p.129(b): © Arcaid Images/Alamy; p.129(c): © D. Hurst/Alamy; p.129(d): © Anki21/Shutterstock; p.129(e): © Woodley Photographic/Alamy; p.129(f): © Elnur/Shutterstock; p.129(g): © Steve Gorton/Getty; p.129(h): © Susanna Price/Getty; p.132(TL): © Jochen Tack/Alamy; p.132(TR): © Franz-Marc Frei/ Corbis/ p.132(B): © James Davies; p.133: © Clearview/Alamy; pp.140/141: © Richard I'Anson/Getty; p.148(a): © Olive Hoffmann/Shutterstock; p.148(b): rvsolft/Shutterstock; p.148(c): © Preto Perola/Shutterstock; p.148(d): © Richard Peterson/Shutterstock; p.148(e): © John Foto/Shutterstock; p.128(f): © Piliphoto/Shutterstock; p.148(g): © Ivageorgieva/Shutterstock; p.148(h): © Volosina/Shutterstock; p.148(i): © Alaettin Yildiram/Shutterstock; p.148(j): © Meelena/Shutterstock; p.148(k): © Aleksey Troshin/Shutterstock; pp.158/159: © Paul Souders/Corbis; p.162(L): © Anders Blomqvist/Getty; p.162(C): © Aleksander Todorovic/Shutterstock; p.162(R): © Jonathan Hewitt/Alamy; p.166(TL): Juniors Bildarchiv GmbH/Alamy; p.166(TR): HP Canada/Alamy; p.166(BL): TNWA Photography; p.166(BR): © Danita Delimont/Alamy; p.169(TL):© Farlap/Alamy; p.169(BL): © Winifried Wisniewski/Corbis; p.169(R): © Keren Su/Corbis; pp.176/177: © Ellen van Bodegon/Getty; p.181(TL): © Chris Batson/Alamy; p.181(TR): © Geo Martinez/Shutterstock; p.181(BL): © Marek Stepan/Alamy; p.181(BR): © Maurice Savage/Alamy; p.185(TL): © Jeff Cook/Corbis/ p.185(TR): © Alan Schein/Corbis; p.185(BL): © Tim McGuire/Corbis; p.185(BC): © Maria Cazia Casella/ Alamy; p.185(BR): © Alistair Laning/Alamy; p.188(L): Stockbyte/Getty; p.188(R): © Martin Bond/Alamy; p.191(L): © Samuel Borges/Shutterstock; p.191(R): © Andres/ Shutterstock; p.195(R): Jupiter Images/Getty; p.195(TL): © Robert Harding Picture Library/Getty; p.195(TR): © Philipus/Alamy; p.195(BL): © Syaochka/ Alamy; p.195(BR): RedChopSticks/Shutterstock; p.198(T): © Lourens Smak/ Alamy; p.198(B): Hemis/Alamy; p.197(TL): © Yang Liu/Corbis/ p.197(T): © David Moore/Alamy; p.197(B): © Gilliane Tedder/Getty.

All videos stills by kind permission of © Discovery Communications LLC 2014

## Illustrations

Fiona Gowen pp 76, 82, 83; Ben Hasler (NB Illustration) pp 19, 108; Oxford Designers & Illustrators pp 16, 34, 35, 40, 76 (top), 78, 131, 136, 142, 160; Martin Sanders (Beehive Illustration) pp 17, 73, 178

## Dictionary

Cambridge dictionaries are the world's most widely used dictionaries for learners of English. Available at three levels (Cambridge Essential English Dictionary, Cambridge Learner's Dictionary and Cambridge Advanced Learner's Dictionary), they provide easy-to-understand definitions, example sentences, and help in avoiding typical mistakes. The dictionaries are also available online at dictionary.cambridge.org. © Cambridge University Press, reproduced with permission.

## Corpus

Development of this publication has made use of the Cambridge English Corpus (CEC). The CEC is a multi-billion word computer database of contemporary spoken and written English. It includes British English, American English and other varieties of English. It also includes the Cambridge Learner Corpus, developed in collaboration with Cambridge English Language Assessment. Cambridge University Press has built up the CEC to provide evidence about language use that helps to produce better language teaching materials.

Picture research by Alison Prior.

Typeset by emc design ltd.